PREPARING FOR A FEDERAL JURY TRIAL

Hon. Willie J. Epps, Jr.

AMERICAN BAR ASSOCIATION
Judicial Division

Cover design by Mary Anne Kulchawik/ABA Design

Printed in the United States of America.

27 26 25 24 23 5 4 3 2 1

ISBN 978-1-63905-321-6

Contents

Acknowledgments

The idea for this book was cultivated during various conversations with my friend, Judge Herbert B. Dixon Jr., a senior judge on the Superior Court of the District of Columbia. I first met Judge Dixon while serving with him on the editorial board of *The Judges' Journal* magazine, where he is the technology columnist. I would not have undertaken this project but for his encouragement and mentorship.

The manuscript for this book was written during COVID-19, the international pandemic that has changed the ways we live, work, and play. I am grateful to my wife, Mischa, and daughter, Cambridge, for giving me love and inspiration during those historic, difficult times, and the space I needed on countless evenings and weekends to finalize this book.

Thanks to the ABA Judicial Division Book Editorial Board for recommending this book for publication. Thanks also to the editors and production staff at the American Bar Association for professional copyediting. The changes and corrections recommended have made this work significantly better.

I learned the fundamentals of conducting jury trials as a student in Trial Advocacy Workshop at Harvard Law School in the early 1990s. My knowledge of and interest in jury trial work grew significantly following law school while serving as an Air Force Judge Advocate General (JAG) prosecutor, and later as an Area Defense Counsel, trying dozens of courts-martial. My trial skills increased greatly as a partner at Shook, Hardy & Bacon LLP, in Kansas City, where I tried product liability, employment, and federal criminal cases to verdict.

I am grateful to the trial lawyers who taught me so much along the way: Professor Charles J. Ogletree Jr., Lt. Col. Mark D. Pollard (ret.), Lt. Col. Larry D. McRell (ret.), Col. Will A. Gunn (ret.), Larry D. Hale, John W. Kurtz, and Robert T. Adams.

As a federal judge, I now have a different vantage point during jury trials. My sincerest thanks to my judicial colleagues here in the Western District of Missouri who take my calls when I have questions and allow me to observe their court proceedings whenever I want.

Thanks to my parents, Drs. Willie and Barbara Epps, for believing in me when I declared, at the age of nine, my intention to become a lawyer. Because of their unconditional love and support, I have been blessed to spend much of my professional life in and around the courtroom.

This book is dedicated to my father, a nationally recognized expert in early childhood education and former Director of the East St. Louis Campus of Southern Illinois University-Edwardsville (SIUE), who died on December 27, 2022, in St. Louis County, Missouri, following a stroke. He was 76.

About the Author

The Honorable Willie J. Epps Jr. is a U.S. Magistrate Judge for the Western District of Missouri and sits in Jefferson City. Judge Epps was born in Mississippi and raised in Missouri. He is a graduate of Amherst College and Harvard Law School, where he teaches annually at Harvard's Trial Advocacy Workshop. He earned his LLM degree in Judicial Studies at Duke University School of Law.

He began his legal career as a trial lawyer in service to our country as a U.S. Air Force Judge Advocate, Special Assistant U.S. Attorney, and Assistant Special Counsel for the Waco Investigation. Later, he was a trial lawyer and partner at two law firms and head of litigation for a financial services company.

Judge Epps is a Fellow of the American College of Trial Lawyers. He serves as Chair of the ABA National Conference of Federal Trial Judges. Prior to being appointed a federal judge, Judge Epps was listed in *The Best Lawyers in America* and *Missouri & Kansas Super Lawyers*.

Introduction

Federal court can be a dangerous place for inexperienced or unprepared counsel. The stakes are usually high, and court rules can be comprehensive and confusing. Given the small number of civil and criminal cases that make it to trial these days, federal court also can be somewhat mysterious.

Why This Book Has Been Written

This book was written to share with you proven trial strategies and techniques that were taught to me and will help you be prepared for your next federal jury trial. This book is for any lawyer interested in developing or enhancing trial advocacy skills at the federal level.

I have been fortunate to spend most of my professional career in and around the courtroom, first as a practicing trial lawyer and now as a federal trial judge. Whatever success I have had during the last quarter century is a direct result of professors, mentors, and senior colleagues providing much needed guidance and advice along the way.

I fell in love with trial work in the early 1990s as a 2L in Harvard's Trial Advocacy Workshop (TAW), an intensive course in trial analysis, skills, and techniques taught by leading academics, practitioners, and judges from across the country. For the first weeks of TAW, we students met in classrooms to conduct trial advocacy exercises, focusing on case theory, direct examination, cross examination, opening statement, and closing argument, leading to simulated bench trials that were critiqued by trial advisors and judges. The course culminated with simulated jury trials in actual state and federal courtrooms throughout Boston and Cambridge. It was quite humbling having mock jurors from the local middle schools and high schools decide whether the fictitious client won or lost the case and make comments afterward about the trial skills exhibited during the mock trial. Months following TAW, as a member of the Harvard Legal Aid Bureau, the oldest student-run legal aid organization in the United States, I got the opportunity to apply newly learned trial skills to actual real-world litigation, representing indigent individuals, under the supervision of clinical instructors.

Following law school graduation and passing the Missouri bar, I found myself on active duty at the Air Force Judge Advocate General's (JAG) School, at Maxwell Air Force Base in Montgomery, Alabama, learning how to try courts-martial. Fulfilling the military service commitment I had incurred through participation in the Air Force Reserve Officers' Training Corps (ROTC) program as an undergraduate, instruction at the JAG School furthered my desire to do jury trial work, which I was able to do shortly after arriving at my first duty station at Goodfellow Air Force Base in San Angelo, Texas.

A mentor once told me that to be a trial lawyer you must try cases. If that observation is true, the U.S. Air Force clearly made me a trial lawyer during my four years of active-duty service. I prosecuted and defended military service members in dozens of courts-martial from Texas, New Mexico, Wyoming, and California to Massachusetts, Colorado, and Nebraska. Criminal charges ranged from theft, absent without leave (AWOL), and illegal drug possession and use to sexual assault and conduct unbecoming of an officer. Prior to my first trial as a young officer, I was terrified. What happens if defense counsel objects during my opening statement or when I attempt to introduce key exhibits? What if my star witnesses fall apart on the witness stand? How do I make sure I admit evidence that satisfies every element of the alleged crime? Fortunately, my first chief of military justice, Captain Mark D. Pollard (now retired as a lieutenant colonel), spent evenings and weekends coaching me on various aspects of trial practice. He taught me how to organize my trial notebook, get a document admitted into evidence, and write out, word for word, an opening and closing. After all these years, I am still grateful for Mark's mentorship. In the chapters that follow, some of the concepts I first learned on a small military base 25 years ago are discussed in some form in hopes that you will win your next federal jury trial.

As you may know, courts-martial are governed by the Uniform Code of Military Justice and Military Rules of Evidence, which are based on and mirror the Federal Rules of Evidence. So, the first time I saw the actual Federal Rules of Evidence being applied at a high level was in 2000, during my service as an Assistant Special Counsel for the Waco Investigation, when my boss, former U.S. Senator Jack Danforth, asked me to observe the Branch Davidian civil jury trial held in the U.S. Courthouse in Waco, Texas. The Davidians sought $675 million against the U.S. government. In a victory for the government, the jury found that federal officials, including the Federal Bureau of Investigation (FBI) and the Federal Bureau of Alcohol, Tobacco, and Firearms (ATF), were not responsible for the deaths of nearly 80 Branch Davidians who were killed in the 1993 raid and standoff at the Davidian complex near Waco. To most people, the civil lawsuit represented a six-year legal battle that eventually became a vastly publicized assessment of the government's trustworthiness. To me, however, that lawsuit represented additional affirmation that I would try cases for a living, preferably in federal court, following government service.

After four years in the Air Force and two years on the Waco Investigation, I became a lawyer in private practice, finding it exceedingly difficult to get into federal court on a regular basis until, that is, I raised my hand to serve on the Criminal Justice Act (CJA) Panel for the U.S. District Court for the Western District of Missouri. My first CJA case to make it to a jury involved allegations of guns and drugs and lasted eight days. My last CJA case, a decade later, involved allegations of securities fraud and was tried before a jury over a five-week period. The skills I developed handling court-appointed criminal matters helped me with my civil trial practice in both federal and state courts. It also helped me with my transition from trial lawyer to trial judge, where I have presided over numerous civil jury trials.

What It Takes to Win

The best prepared lawyer usually wins. Winning may mean receiving the desired verdict. It may also mean receiving an adverse jury verdict, but the right trial record created to win on appeal. Or it may mean outstanding trial advocacy for a client who had an unwinnable case to begin with but wanted their day in court.

I have worked with and seen the very best lawyers in action. Some of them appear before me today. They are always incredibly well prepared. They know the facts of the case and the case law that governs. They are civil and they play fair.

Should You Watch Others in Trial?

Yes, you should watch others in trial. As a lawyer in private practice, I periodically took time away from client matters to watch jury trials being conducted in state and federal courts. Now as a federal trial judge, I visit the courtrooms of colleagues, from time to time, when jury trials are being conducted. I learn a lot by watching others. I take notes about what is being done correctly, and I write down mistakes made in hopes that I do not make the same ones in the future. I tell younger members of the profession that they will always remember the mistakes they see other lawyers make, which, hopefully, will be a learning experience that teaches them never to make the same mistake.

Observational learning has proven to be a powerful tool for retaining information and modeling future behavior. So, when you hear that a really good lawyer has an upcoming jury trial, carve time out of your busy schedule to watch the trial from start to finish. If you cannot take the time to watch the entire trial, I highly recommend that you prioritize by picking important key phases of trial to observe. Some say trials are lost and won during voir dire. I tend to agree with that theory, and so I suggest watching as much of jury selection as your schedule allows. Others believe that opening statements can determine the winner. Agreeing that this phase sets the tone for the entire trial, you should make time to watch. Consider being in the courtroom during key witness testimony or when the parties argue jury instructions. Watching others in trial will help you improve your advocacy skills greatly.

You Should Talk with Experienced Lawyers

Sitting at the feet of experienced trial lawyers can be invaluable. Identify a few men and women in your world who have substantial trial experience. Ask each of them for an hour or so of their time to discuss trial strategy and tactics. Offer to take them out to lunch so that they can recount trial war stories. Ask if you can borrow trial notebooks they have used in past trials.

Being seated across from an experienced trial lawyer for just one short hour can make the difference between winning and losing your next federal jury trial. I vividly remember moments during my trial lawyer career when a more experienced trial lawyer told me about trial concepts I was not familiar with that, going forward, had a material impact on the way I presented evidence to juries.

For the trial-mentoring sessions to be successful, you need to meet with experienced trial lawyers while disconnected from your phone and other matters. You need to really listen to them and find inspiration and motivation when they explain what they love about being a trial lawyer. Please do not limit yourself to lawyers on one side of the "v." Talk to both plaintiff lawyers and defense counsel. Meet with both prosecutors and defenders. For example, when I was a partner at a large law firm in the Midwest, my most important trial mentor was a plaintiff's lawyer operating a firm with just one other lawyer.

Your trial mentor may not look like you, think like you, or practice law in your area of expertise. Be open to trial lawyers from every vantage point and take good notes about the trial concepts they find most important. Ask them about the biggest mistakes and successes they have seen during trial. Ask them how best to connect with jurors and the judge. Inquire about trying cases with civility. Discuss how best to introduce evidence and utilize technology throughout trial.

Second Chairing to Get Experience

As a military prosecutor, I second-chaired a jury trial before being allowed to lead. My JAG mentors would allow me to help with jury selection, deliver the opening statement, and handle a few witnesses. Occasionally, I was asked to take the lead on drafting proposed jury instructions and argue them before the court.

Early in my career in private practice, especially during a phase when I was a solo practitioner, I would beg and plead with other lawyers to allow me to second chair jury trials when they had a case on the brink of trial. I learned a great deal being seated at counsel's table, taking notes during voir dire, helping to organize exhibits, and reading deposition transcripts to jurors when asked. It would have been nice if my civilian mentors had allowed me to handle witnesses, but I took what I could get.

Find lawyers who have cases set for trial and ask if you can help in any way. Getting a chance to just sit at counsel's table during a jury trial is invaluable experience. Getting a chance to conduct a direct or cross examination of a witness is even better. But anytime you can be in a courtroom and get on your feet in front of a judge or jury is a big deal.

Reading Trial Transcripts

Prior to taking my first significant depositions as a lawyer at a large law firm, I gathered 20 or so deposition transcripts and studied them intently. Thereafter, I drafted my deposition questions based on what I had learned from my research of past depositions and the particular facts of the pending case. The same can be done to prepare for trial. Look for and gather as many trial transcripts as you can find and read them closely. Pay attention to the way lawyers organize their statements, questions, and objections. It is preferable to find transcripts in the subject area of your upcoming trial. For example, if you are preparing to prosecute an employment case, it makes the most sense to study transcripts of employment cases that have been tried in recent years. If you are defending a criminal case involving allegations of methamphetamine possession, distribution, and use, it is better to review recent trial transcripts of federal drug cases.

Establish a PACER (Public Access to Court Electronic Records) account to search for and download, or print, trial transcripts. Also, reach out to trial lawyers, including your federal public defender, for transcripts of recent cases.

Watching Trials on Television

I'm not referring to watching *Law and Order* or any other scripted TV show drama. I am referring to real trials presented by television broadcast or streamed over the Internet. When I was in law school, the so-called Trial of the Century, *The People vs. O.J. Simpson*, was televised from beginning to end, changing the way national networks and cable television channels cover high-profile legal disputes. Today, a wealth of resources is available to watch jury trial coverage, ranging from YouTube and Court TV to cable news channels and national newspaper websites. Watching others try cases before juries can help you further develop your jury trial skills. Televised jury trials are conducted in state court since television coverage is not allowed in federal courtrooms.

Obtaining Judge's Rules of Trial

The rules of trial give counsel and the parties guidance on how the judge will conduct the jury trial. The rules of trial that I have in place in my courtroom are similar to what my judicial colleagues use in my District and across the country. My standing rules cover technology, courtroom conduct, exhibits, voir dire, objections, jury questions, opening statement and closing argument, and communication with chambers.

With respect to technology, I require trial counsel to test the equipment in the courtroom more than one week prior to trial. This is a requirement, not an option. I firmly believe that there should not be any technology glitches during trial that could have been avoided with proper preparation. I let counsel know that they may schedule a time to test courtroom equipment with an information technology specialist. I also require counsel to understand how to properly impeach a witness from the podium using the tech equipment. This avoids the inconvenience of approaching a witness with a paper copy of a report or deposition, as well as the confusion in court and difficulty for the court reporter. Finally, counsel must identify whether there will be one technician displaying exhibits for all parties or separate technicians for each party.

Prior to trial, counsel must designate for the court lead counsel and identify all individuals who will sit at counsel's table. For the sake of the court reporter and the jury, I insist that counsel stand at the podium or at counsel's table and speak into the microphone when on the record. I remind counsel that the court reporter can only transcribe one speaker at a time and to be mindful at all times not to speak over others, especially when questioning witnesses and during sidebars.

Civility is important to me. Counsel should always be professional and respectful, including moments when the jury is not present or when the court is off the record. Counsel must avoid dramatic facial expressions and gestures when the judge or opposing counsel are speaking. Counsel are ordered to address individuals, including opposing counsel and witnesses, by their last names and the appropriate title (e.g., Dr., Mr., or Ms.).

With respect to exhibits, my trial order requires counsel to confer with opposing counsel prior to trial and to come to an agreement concerning whether certain exhibits may be used during opening statements. If so, they must review and agree on those exhibits in advance, which should be marked individually. If only one page or portion of evidence will be admitted, it should have its own exhibit number. Counsel should not attempt to admit only a piece of an exhibit or to use "subexhibit" numbers. (For example, counsel may not admit page 63 of Exhibit 29. If the entire exhibit is not to be admitted, it must be divided.) Counsel must check the exhibit list carefully for errors prior to trial. Mistakes in exhibit numbering only slow down trial tempo and are a waste of time for all involved. Counsel should confer with opposing counsel to come to an agreement concerning what exhibits will be admitted at trial. Counsel may jointly preadmit these exhibits to the court, with an accompanying list of exhibits on which no consensus can be reached by the parties.

Regarding voir dire, the court asks all questions during voir dire unless counsel, during pretrial hearing, requests extensive participation in the jury selection process. Voir dire questions must be submitted to the court before trial. The court will notify both parties of the final questions prior to jury selection. If a potential juror requires further, individual examination, counsel will have an opportunity to question that specific juror outside the hearing of the rest of the jury panel.

To object at trial, I require counsel to stand and speak into the microphone, "Your honor, objection." The court will ask counsel to state the basis briefly. I require counsel to use discretion, understanding that the jury is listening. Counsel should not create a prejudicial error by giving a speech with an objection in the presence of the jury. Sidebars allowing for argument on objections are very limited.

I am in the minority of federal trial judges who allow jury questions during civil trials. With agreement of the parties, the jury can ask written questions of every witness who testifies in court. Some judges permit jurors to submit questions over the objection of counsel.

In a sidebar, both parties may choose to object to questions before they are presented to the witness. The court will read a question and poll lead counsel for each party. Counsel must state whether there is an objection or whether there is agreement that the question should be asked and counsel must provide a brief basis. Counsel are not allowed to offer lengthy explanation. Even though jurors' handwritten questions are docketed, the reporter's transcript will reflect the judge's reading of the question, and, obviously, the objections and the rephrased question as posed to the jury by the judge.

My trial order states that each party will have 30 minutes for the opening statement and 30 minutes for the closing argument. If the parties agree, the jury will be instructed on the law prior to an opening statement and again before closing argument.

With respect to rules governing communication with chambers, I require counsel to pose questions regarding scheduling and the court's Electronic Filing System to my courtroom deputy. For other questions, trial lawyers may contact one of my law clerks.

While many of my judicial colleagues have similar rules, none of us have identical rules. Accordingly, it is very important for you to track down the rules of your trial judge so that you understand exactly what your judge requires and expects.

Getting Started

These are just some thoughts to help you get started, especially if you are newer to trial practice. If you are decades into your career, perhaps what is written here will remind you of the basics and make you better. Next, I will challenge you to get more organized and focused, and I will outline what I think is important as you prepare to try a case. Part II of the book profiles my conversations with top trial lawyers and how they succeed at trial. Part III is my model trial notebook that can be a resource during trial preparation.

I wish you much success with your next federal jury trial.

Part I
Jury Trial Phases

1
Trial Preparation

Over the years, I have observed a countless number of talented trial lawyers. Some have worn military uniforms; most have not. Among the best have been both men and women, of various racial backgrounds, of varying styles, some with swagger, a few with no detectable ego. Most have been well dressed; others have been complete slobs. But all these great trial lawyers have been prepared, organized, and focused.

As a result of being around the best, I have developed my own rules and viewpoints on trials and provide them here. While my focus has generally been on the federal trial court, these perspectives undoubtably have wider applicability. The most striking of these perspectives follow below.

Preparation, Preparation, Preparation

To be successful, a trial attorney must have a grasp of the entire casefile, memorizing as many witness statements, expert reports, and facts of the case as possible. My former Dowd Bennett law partner, Jim Bennett, has a near photographic memory, enabling him to recall specific exhibit numbers and the contents thereof, as well as actual deposition statements verbatim. While I have never seen super lawyer David Boies in trial, I understand he may have a photographic memory, despite his public denials, enabling him to catalogue deposition testimony and a timeline of events in his mind without referring to one single page of paper.

Photographic memory or not, proper preparation is essential. The late, great Johnnie Cochran once said that the biggest lesson he learned in life is that "[t]here is no substitute for hard work and that three keys to successes are preparation, preparation and preparation."[1] Ted Wells of Paul Weiss is known to hole up in a hotel room for weeks studying the casefile before trial. Like all the leading trial lawyers, he prides himself on being the most prepared when he enters the courtroom, knowing that no one understands the facts of the case better.

For any type of jury trial, mastering the facts of the case allows trial lawyers to make informed assessments about case themes and theories. My observation, though, is that the most thorough preparation, while necessary and helpful, does not guarantee the desired verdict. Proper preparation and command of the case facts cannot overcome instances when the fact pattern is simply bad for your client. That said, your trial preparation should be extensive, giving your client the best odds of being successful at trial.

The Law

While the jurors are judges of the facts of the case, the trial judge is the ultimate authority on the law. Excellent trial lawyers strive to know the law better than the judge, often drafting a set of jury instructions months in advance of trial and researching appellate guidance with respect to the most essential instructions and their elements. Focusing on each element early in the case also allows lawyers to categorize anticipated evidence under each relevant element.

Unfortunately, most lawyers drop the ball at trial when it comes to the law. First, many will ask a junior associate to draft instructions—for the very first time—on the eve of the jury instructions conference. Second, the junior associate, with little training and minimal

---

[1] Monique R. Brown, *Let My Work Speak for Me: Johnnie Cochran Reviews the Trials and Triumphs of His Career*, 10 Network Journal 4 at 46 (Jan. 31, 2003), https://www.proquest.com/openview/3adfb1c118ae7775411dbed0c510a875/1?cbl=43721&pq-origsite=gscholar&parentSessionId=VLE49daAY2zzA6Odqswprt3EDtGrVG%2BXxh%2B0Egvxxbs%3D.

guidance, may be asked at the last minute to argue jury instructions to the court. Third, lawyers often fail to preserve the trial record for appeal when the court denies motions to include certain proposed instructions.

A prepared lawyer, whether lead counsel or junior associate, can make a gigantic difference during a jury instructions conference. When judges are crafting the most appropriate instructions for a case, they, in fact, enjoy engaging with well-prepared lawyers and find it difficult to engage underprepared counsel.

As soon as you think a case is headed for a jury trial, you should start drafting the jury instructions. When I wanted to be laser focused on what must be proven at trial to win, for certain cases I drafted instructions earlier than that, before even taking the first deposition. Too many senior lawyers delegate this important task to a junior lawyer and often at the last minute. To give your client the best chance of winning at trial, it makes the most sense for lead counsel to spend considerable time drafting and reviewing jury instructions well in advance of trial.

Hopefully, you are trying your next federal jury trial in a jurisdiction where model jury instructions exist. I am a judge who sits in the Western District of Missouri, which is part of the Eighth Circuit. Here, we have both the *Manual of Model Criminal Jury Instructions for the District Courts of the Eighth Circuit* and the *Manual of Model Civil Jury Instructions for the District Courts of the Eighth Circuit.*

Our model jury instructions have been written and revised by committees of federal judges, trial lawyers, and law professors to help judges communicate more successfully with juries. Each manual is designed to give judges and lawyers a model of clear, short, and plain-language instructions tailored to lead to juror comprehension. The manuals are not designed to be the only way of properly instructing a jury. That is to say, the model instructions are not mandatory or binding, and they may be modified.

My experience is that these manuals do an excellent job of anticipating the needs of the parties in most disputes that come before our federal courts here in the Midwest. I do not assume, however, that these model instructions will be appropriate for every case that makes it to trial. Because each case is unique, instructions should be crafted to fit the facts in each case. If there is a need to alter an instruction, you should frame the additional language as simply as possible, keeping your sentences short, clear, and concise. The last thing any good trial lawyer wants to do is recommend to the court language that will confuse jurors.

The good news is that most circuits have model jury instructions. If you find that certain instructions in your jurisdiction are not as strong or as well written as you would like, look to the model instructions from other circuits first. You should also look to case law within and outside your jurisdiction that may frame an issue better than the model instructions.

Organization

For most great trial lawyers, organization starts with a robust trial notebook. A solid trial notebook may be your passport to victory and your key to being better organized than opposing counsel. The trial notebook is divided to act as a roadmap for the trial of the case from pretrial conference and jury selection to jury verdict. In my years as a lawyer, I would use 11 tabs in the trial notebook both to prepare for trial and to follow throughout the jury trial process.

Tab One of my ideal trial notebook contains all pretrial matters: Rules of Jury Trial, Pretrial Checklist, Motions in Limine, and Other Motions.

Tab Two should contain your proposed voir dire, proposed witness list, proposed exhibit list, and proposed jury instructions.

Tab Three should contain your opposing counsel's proposed voir dire, proposed witness list, proposed exhibit list, and proposed jury instructions.

Tab Four is labeled Jury Selection; it should contain chart/strikes and juror profile.

Tab Five should contain your opening statement.

Tab Six is your opponent's case.

Tab Seven in a criminal case (in which you are defending) should contain your Motion for Judgment of Acquittal at Close of Government's Case. Tab Seven in a civil case (in which you are defending) should contain your Motion for Judgment at Close of the Plaintiff's Case.

Tab Eight in a criminal case (in which you are defending) is your client's case.

Tab Nine in a criminal case (in which you are defending) should contain your Motion for Judgment of Acquittal at Close of All Evidence. Tab Nine in a civil case (in which you are defending) should contain your Motion for Judgment at Close of All Evidence.

Tab Ten should be labeled Jury Instruction Conference.

Tab Eleven should contain your closing argument.

Start building your trial notebook as soon as you know the case is a good candidate for trial. Your notebook may be in physical form such as a three-ring notebook or virtual. Since the jury instructions are the law of the case and vitally important, start drafting them first and placing them in the trial notebook.

Case Theory

Once you have your jury instructions drafted, you will have an excellent idea of the hill you must climb at trial. Now is the time to identify your case theory. A case theory is a coherent story of what has happened in the case and why your client should recover at trial, involving factual theories and legal theories.

In a criminal case, you might hear the following:

> The defendant grew up in a tough part of the city. He hung out with gang members for protection. He saw things that a young man should not see, and he has done things he is not proud of. But he has never sold drugs or conspired to sell drugs. The cooperating witnesses in this case are lying to get out of jail, but you will learn the truth. He is not guilty of the charges.

In a civil case, you might hear:

> The accident was caused by plaintiff misusing the farm equipment, which performed properly. The farmer operated the equipment in an area of the property that was too steep for the machine. He operated the equipment on a slope exceeding 40 degrees when the manufacturer limited its use to a maximum of 20 degrees. During the rollover, the roof performed

as expected. The head injury was caused by the farmer being out of position and wearing the seat belt improperly. The jury should decide this case in favor of the defendant.

Case Theme

Next, craft a case theme that captures the case theory. The theme may be one word or a short phrase. The goal should be to come up with something that is short and memorable. You want the jurors talking about your theme during deliberations. I have used the following themes:

- The defendant is no Boy Scout, but he is not a drug dealer either.
- The car fire was started by a faulty battery, not the alternator.
- The defendant is a barracks thief.
- To whom much is given, much is required.
- The defendant must take personal responsibility.
- The vehicle performed as expected when the driver fell asleep.
- No competent expert can claim the drug at issue is defective.
- The company did not put profits over people.
- The defendant did not violate labor sourcing laws.
- No one is above the law.
- The doctor could not identify structures and violated a rule by continuing to operate.
- No means no.

I have heard the following themes:

- Some people will do anything for love.
- Mo money, mo problems.
- Money makes the world go around.
- He took what he wanted.

Timeline

A timeline is essentially a visual of your case theory and theme. It is a listing of important events that help illustrate and prove your client's point of view. The timeline may be written on posterboard or presented to the jury electronically. The more factual and neutral the better. If the entries are argumentative, objections are likely to be sustained. Using the very same demonstrative exhibit in opening and closing can be effective. It is a great way to signal to the jury that you did not mislead them initially. In closing, you can point to each entry and remind them about which witness or exhibit made that fact true.

Trial Memorandum

Most judges, along with their law clerks, find a trial memorandum helpful. A trial memorandum reflects what a party believes the evidence will show. Key witnesses are listed and anticipated testimony is summarized. Important exhibits are discussed. Relevant case law is applied to the anticipated facts. Most importantly, a good trial brief raises legal issues that a party anticipates may surface at trial.

In a drug conspiracy case, the government typically calls a number of witnesses, who participated in the conspiracy, to testify about their activities in the conspiracy, as well as to enlighten the jury about how the conspiracy worked and who bought and sold illegal substances. Usually, those witnesses have pled guilty via a plea agreement pledging cooperation with the government.

In such a case, it probably makes sense for one or both parties to remind the court in a trial memo of the rule within the circuit that governs evidence of a codefendant's guilty plea to the same offense. Is such evidence permissible? What if the evidence is elicited as substantive proof of the defendant's guilt? In most jurisdictions, including the Eighth Circuit, such evidence would be excluded in that circumstance. But it is admissible to show a witness's acknowledgment of participation in the drug offense or to reflect on their credibility. In such circumstances, the jury is instructed that the evidence is received for this purpose alone and that they are not to infer the guilt of the defendant or defendants on that fact. Acknowledging the guilty pleas of co-conspirators in such a case, along with a limiting instruction, allows jurors to know about the context of the drug crimes and events that help explain the context. It is best practice to suggest limiting instructions that should instruct the jury not to consider such a guilty plea as any evidence of this defendant's guilt. It should also instruct that the jury may consider such a guilty plea only for the purpose of determining how much, if at all, they should rely on a witness's testimony.

Drug conspiracy cases also involve evidence of tools of the drug trade. When parties anticipate there will be expert testimony that conspirators in the case were likely to communicate with cell phones, possess heat-sealing equipment and packaging used to package drugs for distribution, and maintain large amounts of cash, it is wise to cite case law in your trial memo explaining whether such evidence is relevant in a narcotics prosecution and whether such is evidence of illegal dealings and ill-gotten gains.

Under what circumstances may the United States offer evidence showing unexplained wealth for a defendant? When is such evidence relevant? The party that best explains case law to the court in a trial memo will have an advantage at trial with the judge and the judge's law clerks.

Ideal Juror

Is your ideal juror highly educated or a high school dropout? Young or old? Urban or rural? Is your ideal juror familiar or unfamiliar with the concepts that will be discussed at trial?

Pretrial Conference

Take the pretrial conference seriously. This is your chance to raise issues that will be important to your case and to receive, perhaps, preliminary guidance from your judge about their opinions. Have a pretrial list of issues to raise. Are there any pending motions requiring the court's attention? If so, remind the court that you need a ruling and explain why that timely ruling is necessary. Confirm the number of witnesses you intend to call, and make sure your opponent informs the court witnesses that the other side intends to call. Will the parties be invoking "the rule on witnesses"? If so, please remind the judge and opposing counsel that witnesses will not be allowed in the courtroom until it is time for their testimony. Also, place on the record that witnesses are not to be shown a transcript of trial testimony prior to taking the witness stand. How much time does each side get for voir dire, if any, following the court's questioning? Will proposed questions need to be submitted in advance of trial? Who will be conducting voir dire for each party? Who will be seated at counsel's table throughout trial? Will a lawyer or party representative be absent at any point during trial? If so, make sure the judge is aware of the absence. If you think your opponent will exploit the absence of counsel or party representative, try to get a preliminary ruling that opposing counsel cannot comment on the absence in front of the jury.

How many jurors will be seated? In a criminal case, it is customary to seat 12 and to pick a couple of alternatives. In a civil case, at least 6 must be seated, but many judges will choose to seat more, up to 12. Will there be alternates seated or will every juror get to deliberate? Will the parties do challenges for cause and then pick the top 22 perspective jurors? How many strikes will each side get? Is the number 4? If so, that is a total of 8 preemptory strikes for the parties. That should leave you with 12 jurors, and 2 alternates.

Think about the opening statements. How long will each side get? Thirty minutes each? Will counsel be able to display preadmitted exhibits to the jury during opening? Will counsel be permitted to use a demonstrative exhibit? Must the demonstrative aid be shown to the other side before opening? If so, how far in advance? What if there is an objection to the demonstrative exhibit? Will the court be able to take that issue up well in advance of the opening?

Depending on the kind of case being tried, these questions just scratch the surface. For instance, if you are trying a serious injury case, inquire whether the injured party needs to be present for voir dire or opening. Check with the judge about how best to move a wheelchair-bound person around the courtroom. Will any large demonstrative exhibit be used during trial and when expert witnesses testify? If so, must the other side be able to inspect beforehand? How will the demonstrative exhibit be moved into the courthouse, generally, and into the courtroom, specifically?

Be sure to discuss start and stop times throughout trial. Will there be a morning break or an afternoon break? If so, at what times? Will the jury ever be asked to stay late if there is a witness who needs to finish testimony that day? Or will the witness have to come back the next day to finish if they go past the deadline?

Confirm with judge and court staff how exhibits should be premarked. Inquire into whether counsel must request to approach a witness. How should counsel publish admitted documents and photographs to the jury? Are jurors allowed to handle exhibits physically, or must counsel publish electronically? If the case involves a weapon, seek the court's guidance on how to handle this fact in the courtroom.

Co-Counsel

When practical, you should try your case with co-counsel. Two sets of eyes are better than one. Additional counsel can assist with case research, take notes during voir dire, handle less important witnesses, and, if properly prepared, argue jury instructions.

During my days as a trial lawyer, I insisted on taking one or two younger lawyers to trial. First, I needed the help with pretrial briefing, proposed jury instructions, proposed witness list, and motions in limine. Second, with respect to jury selection, I found that my co-counsel would often observe reactions, body language, and nonverbal responses from perspective jurors that I would miss while conducting voir dire. Looking back, I am positive that jury selection was more in my own and my client's favor because of contributions from co-counsel. Third, during longer, more significant trials, it can be a relief for lead counsel to have help examining lay witnesses and expert witnesses. That is, if there are 20 witnesses, it is nice to be able to give 3 to 5 to co-counsel. Finally, I believe co-counsel can assist greatly with client control and expectations. As you know, there is so much going on when a jury is seated for trial. To have additional lawyers on the team to shoulder the load can make the difference between being overloaded or carrying a manageable load.

Technology

Most federal courtrooms are equipped with state-of-the-art technology. The equipment exists to help lawyers, judges, and court staff do their jobs more efficiently and effectively. Use it.

Counsel should make a concerted effort to learn how to display documents from a computer system to screens and monitors in the courtroom. Yes, you will want to have hardcopy backup documents in folders and boxes at counsel's table in case technology fails you. But prepare as if you will present most of your exhibits via your laptop or tablet and through the monitors in the courtroom. Agreeing with opposing counsel to share a resource to operate the equipment is a plus.

Counsel also should think of creative ways to use the document camera to present evidence at trial. When I started practicing, we used overhead projectors. Now we have the ELMO, a fantastic replacement for that twentieth-century equipment, that counsel should be able to operate with ease to get quality visual persuasiveness out of necessary exhibits. Practice using the ELMO weeks before trial so that you are a pro when you get in front of the jury.

2
Voir Dire

Some trial lawyers claim that cases are won or lost during voir dire. Really good lawyers work hard during jury selection to identify and eliminate potential jurors who harbor bias against their clients. Without serious preparation for the jury selection phase of trial, months and weeks in advance of trial, counsel runs the risk of sabotaging their case before opening statements are even delivered.

Purposes of Jury Selection

In addition to identifying jurors with bias, voir dire is an opportunity for counsel to establish rapport with jurors, introduce key themes and theories of the case, and learn more about jurors' backgrounds, experiences, and beliefs. Being likeable helps lawyers win cases. Jurors tend to fight for people they like. They tend to like lawyers who listen carefully to their answers, give them good eye contact, and appear prepared and comfortable in the courtroom.

Find Out in Advance of Trial If Lawyers Will Participate in Asking Jurors Questions

Voir dire is a part of the jury trial procedure and management at the federal level that is fully and totally within the discretion of the trial judge, though this discretion is not without boundaries. The judge has complete freedom to decide whether to allow or disallow counsel participation in the process. Typically, a judge will make the decision regarding whether to allow counsel's participation shortly before trial. If allowed, the court will generally set guardrails, including which questions may be asked and the length of time each party will have to conduct voir dire. If disallowed, the court is required to ensure voir dire is conducted in such a way that protects the parties from prejudice and permits the parties to judiciously use its peremptory challenges.

A party may argue to conduct voir dire to ensure that a fair and impartial jury is selected. In such cases, a party usually asserts that additional inquiry is needed to weed out jurors exposed to excessive pretrial publicity, bias against a party, harboring racial or gender prejudice, and so on. The burden is on the moving party to convince the trial judge, who is usually armed with proposed questions from both parties, as to why the judge cannot adequately ensure that the jury is impartial and that the parties have the information needed to exercise their challenges. In criminal cases, more and more judges now allow the parties to ask jurors about their biases and experiences, including those against police officers. In doing so, counsel is often permitted to inquire into any biases jurors may have regarding race and policing. A district court abuses its discretion when it denies a party's request to inquire into racial bias only when there is a considerable probability that racial bias is affecting jurors in the case. Courts of appeal have consistently held that the trial judge is in the best position to analyze the demeanor and credibility of prospective jurors.

A party may also argue for individualized voir dire that is private and away from other prospective jurors. We can all agree that it is sometimes difficult to answer invasive questions in front of 40–60 other potential jurors. And while many may concede that individualized voir dire may be superior to current voir dire practices, the real issue is whether there is a constitutional right to such a voir dire. The author is unaware of any circuit court that has required a district court to conduct individualized voir dire.

Drafting a Proposed Voir Dire

Whether the judge intends to conduct the entire voir dire with no follow-up questions from counsel or to conduct voir dire with limited follow-up questions from counsel based on the jurors' prior responses, counsel would be wise to submit all voir dire questions in advance of trial that counsel would ask if allowed to do so.

The proposed voir dire questions in a criminal case are submitted pursuant to Rule 24(a) of the Federal Rules of Criminal Procedure. In a civil case, the proposed voir dire questions are submitted pursuant to Local rules and the judge's memorandum to counsel regarding trial procedures. Counsel should expressly request that the court pursue more detailed questioning if a particular juror's answer reveals that further inquiry is appropriate. In such an instance, counsel should conclude with an inquiry as to whether the particular fact or circumstance would influence the juror in favor of or against either the government or the defense.

Here is the first section of proposed voir dire questions in the court's *introduction* section:

> Good morning to all of you. I want to just tell you, for those of you who have not been through this process before, we will be asking you some questions here. The purpose of the questions is not to be nosey, but just to allow me and also the attorneys in the case to make an informed decision about whether or not you could be fair and impartial as a juror in this particular case. After we ask you these questions, then the lawyers in the case will have a certain number of what we call preemptory challenges that they can exercise, which will excuse some of you. Then some of you will remain as jurors, and those of you who remain will be the jurors who actually serve in this case. Let me explain to you just a little bit about what this case involves.

You should request that the court, in this first section, inform the jury as to whether the case is civil or criminal, identify the parties, and describe the allegations:

> This is a criminal case. All defendants are charged in Count One with Conspiracy to commit Securities Fraud and Wire Fraud. Defendant Dallas Hastie is further charged with Securities Fraud, Aggravated Currency Structuring, Money Laundering,

and Wire Fraud. Defendant Paris Marshall is further charged with Securities Fraud and Wire Fraud. Defendant Louis Houston is further charged with Wire Fraud. Defendant Tokyo Murray is further charged with Money Laundering and Wire Fraud. Defendant Helsinki Robinson is not charged in any additional counts. The defendants have pleaded not guilty. And I should tell you that the indictment is not evidence of any kind against the defendants. It's just a mechanical means by which the case is brought to this court for trial here this morning. The defendants in the case, of course, as I will tell you later as well, begin with a clean slate, with no evidence at all against them.

The second section of your proposed voir dire should focus on *knowledge of the case and participants.* Ask members of the panel if they had heard anything about the case prior to coming to court. Ask if any juror has read, heard, or seen news media or other public reports concerning the case, including in newspapers or on the internet or otherwise. Ask if any juror has any personal knowledge of the charges in the indictment (in a criminal case) or any personal knowledge of the complaint (in a civil case). If so, ask about that personal knowledge and whether that personal knowledge would cause the juror to feel that they could not decide the fact issues of the case fairly and impartially.

Be sure that the court introduces the people who will be involved in the trial. In a criminal case, the prosecutors are usually introduced first and jurors are asked if anyone knows them. The case agent and others seated at the government's table should be introduced and jurors asked if anyone knows the agent or has had any dealings, directly or indirectly, with the case agent or anyone else seated at the government's table.

Furthermore, ask if jurors know any relative, friend, or associate of the prosecutors, the case agent, or anyone seated at the government's table? Announce the name of the U.S. Attorney for the jurisdiction and inquire whether anyone knows the U.S. Attorney or anyone who works for the U.S. Attorney's Office.

Next, the lead defense lawyer should be introduced and jurors asked if anybody knows them. Ask if anyone is familiar with the defense counsel's law firm. The lead defense counsel should be permitted to introduce the defendant and any co-counsel. Inquiry should be made if jurors know, or have had any dealings, directly or indirectly, with the defendant or defense counsel, or with any relative, friend, or associate of the defendant or defense counsel. This process should be repeated for each defense attorney and their client.

Finally, the trial judge should be introduced and panel members asked if anyone knows the judge or if they have had any dealings with the judge, chamber's staff, or judge's family, either directly or indirectly.

The third section of your proposed voir dire should focus on *background, education, and employment.* At this point in the proposed voir dire, the first prospective juror should be asked to stand and state name, age, marital status, educational background, current employment, current employment of spouse, and past jury experience. Repeat with each prospective juror.

Now that jurors have heard what the case is about and what the allegations in the case are, ask if there is anything about those allegations that would prevent any of them from being fair and impartial to both sides in the case. Ask the jurors if they will be able to make their decision in the case based solely on the evidence that they hear in the courtroom.

Next, jurors should be told how many days it will take to try the case. Then they should be asked if that timeline presents any particular scheduling problem for any member of the panel.

Jurors should be asked if any of them has taken undergraduate courses in criminal justice or attended law school, has experience in criminal law, or has any legal training whatsoever, including taking paralegal courses. Ask if any panel member's spouse or family member has experience in criminal law; if so, ask the juror to state the general nature of that experience.

In a criminal case, ask if jurors, close family, or friends ever worked, either formally or informally, or applied for employment with, a law enforcement agency. State that law enforcement agencies include organizations such as the police department, Federal Bureau of Investigation (FBI), Circuit Attorney's or County Prosecutor's Office, U.S. Attorney's Office, U.S. Department of Justice, Central Intelligence Agency (CIA), Internal Revenue Service (IRS), the Securities and Exchange Commission (SEC), Secret Service, Military Police, General

Services Administration (GSA) Guards, private security firms, and the like. Ask if any juror has any bias or prejudice for or against law enforcement.

Ask how many of them (or close friends or relatives) have been employed by any prison, jail, department of corrections, probation office, or parole agency. Ask if anyone (or close friends or relatives) has ever worked for a federal, state, or local court system in any capacity. Also ask if anyone (or close friends or relatives) has ever worked for any entity involved in the case, listing those entities.

The fourth section of your proposed voir dire should focus on *prior jury and litigation experience.* Inquire about whether any member of the jury, a family member, or a close friend has been involved in a criminal or civil trial at the state or federal level. If so, please have these jurors give details. Ask if they were satisfied with the outcome and if the outcome was fair. Ask what the juror thought of the job that the lawyers did. Ask if any member of the panel had served as jury foreperson during trial. Ask if any aspect of that experience would affect their ability to sit as a juror in the pending case. Furthermore, ask whether they would be able to put that past experience aside, consider the evidence in the pending case, and apply the instructions the judge gives them in the instant case. Ask whether any jury member, family member, or close friend ever has had to testify in court or at a deposition. Ask about the circumstances and how they felt about testifying.

It is important to know whether any member of the jury had any unpleasant associations with lawyers, judges or the courts, so ask. If so, ask whether that experience would interfere with their ability to decide this case fairly and impartially.

The fifth section of your proposed voir dire should focus on the *nature of the charges.* First, further describe the evidence that the jurors will hear in the case. In a securities fraud case, ask if the fact that the charges involve the securities industry, investing, or fraud allegedly committed in connection with the securities industry will make it difficult for anyone to render a fair verdict.

Jurors in any case are required to set aside concerns and attitudes about certain issues of case relevance. Jurors in a securities fraud case would be required to set aside concerns and attitudes on general investment issues and decide the case independently and solely on the evidence and the instructions as the court gives them. Ask jurors if they might find that difficult to do. As a follow-up, ask jurors who have invested in securities (such as stocks, bonds, and options) whether their experience as an investor will affect their ability to be fair and impartial in the case. Ask if anyone is an accredited investor or has worked in the securities industry. Lastly, ask whether anyone has served as a director or officer of a public or privately held company. If so, ask whether their experience in that industry would affect their ability to be fair and impartial to both the government and the defendants.

In any case, counsel should explore opinions on government regulations or oversight. In a securities fraud case, ask whether anyone believes that the securities industry should not be regulated by the state or federal government. Ask whether any juror feels that they cannot decide fairly and impartially a case that involves allegations of securities fraud.

Explore whether anyone on the panel is familiar with corporate entities that will appear at trial. In our security fraud hypothetical, ask if anyone is familiar with American Banking. Inquire whether any juror has invested in American Banking. Find out if there is anything about their knowledge of American Banking that would cause anyone to feel that they could not decide fact issues of the case fairly and impartially.

Explore whether anyone on the panel is familiar with people who may testify during trial. Ask if any juror knows, either directly or indirectly, the following individuals who may be called to testify as witnesses or whose names may come up during the trial. The court is then requested to read the names listed on the government's and the defendants' witness lists.

If law enforcement will be involved in your federal trial, explore any bias that may exist. Ask whether any juror, close relative, or close friend has ever been involved or appeared as a witness in any investigation by law enforcement, which would include the SEC and the Missouri Secretary of State's Office in the hypothetical. Ask if anyone feels that federal agent testimony is more likely to be believable or reliable than testimony by another witness. Ask if jurors had to choose who to believe, a federal agent or a witness called by a defendant, how many would be more likely to believe the federal agent because of their role as federal agent. Ask how many agree that, in general, federal agents don't make mistakes.

Members of the panel may form opinions about the lawyers before the jury is seated. Ask if anyone has formed any opinions about either the prosecutor or defense attorneys that would affect them in deciding the case fairly and impartially.

In any criminal case, explore general attitudes about crime. Ask whether anyone has strong feelings about crime. Ask if anyone, whether a family member or a close friend, has been a victim of a crime. Ask if anyone, either a family member or a close friend, has ever been a victim of financial fraud.

In any case that may attract media coverage, explore that issue. If the trial attracts local press attention, ask each juror if they will follow the court's instructions to refrain from viewing or reading any such reports in order to assure a fair trial based only on the evidence presented in the courtroom.

Some members of the panel will not want to serve as jurors. Explore that issue to identify those who want off. Ask whether any member of the panel does not wish to sit on the jury for any reason whatsoever. Ask if anyone has a reason that they would prefer not to sit but would want to keep the reason private.

The sixth section of your proposed voir dire should focus on the *presumption of innocence and burden of proof*. In a criminal case, you should let members of the panel know that they will be instructed at the beginning and conclusion of trial that an indictment is simply an accusation; it is not evidence of anything. To the contrary, all defendants are presumed to be innocent. Thus, each defendant, even though charged, begins the trial with no evidence against them. So the presumption of innocence alone is sufficient to find that each defendant is not guilty and can be overcome only if the government proves, beyond a reasonable doubt, each element of the crimes charged. Ask if anyone feels that each of the defendants should be required to prove their innocence. Ask if anyone feels that the defendants are probably guilty based just on the fact that they have been charged with crimes. Ask whether anyone believes that a person can be falsely accused of a crime. Ask whether any member of the panel has been a victim, or knows somebody who has been a victim, of a false allegation.

In a criminal case, there is no burden on the defendants to prove their innocence. Thus, each individual defendant has the right not to testify. That is, each defendant can remain silent throughout the trial. Ask whether anyone will be disappointed if a defendant decides not to testify. Ask if anyone believes a defendant has an obligation to prove their innocence. Ask if anyone would consider a defendant's failure to testify as evidence of guilt.

In a multi-defendant case, some codefendants may have pleaded guilty to a crime that arose out of the same events for the defendants who are on trial. Tell members of the panel that they cannot consider those guilty pleas as any evidence of these defendants' guilt. Then ask if anyone would feel that, because others pleaded guilty in the case, the defendants on trial must also be guilty.

For criminal cases with more than one defendant, quantify for the members of the panel and state that jurors must give separate consideration to the evidence about each individual defendant. State that each defendant is entitled to be treated separately. Ask if anyone would have trouble considering, separately, each crime charged against each individual defendant.

Let jurors know that they will receive instructions at the end of trial that each of them must make their own conscientious decision regarding guilt or innocence, but only after they have considered all the evidence, discussed it fully with fellow jurors, and listened to the views of fellow jurors. Ask jurors if each of them agrees to make up their own minds individually and return only a verdict to which they agree. Ask if anyone would join a verdict just because the majority of the other jurors favored it, regardless of their personal belief as to the facts.

In a criminal case, the defendant enjoys the presumption, which remains on the defendant throughout the course of the trial, unless and until the triers of fact are convinced beyond a reasonable doubt that the defendant is guilty. The prosecution bears the burden of establishing the guilt of the defendant beyond a reasonable doubt. A reasonable doubt is a doubt based on reason. The defendant is not required to prove innocence. The defendant has the right to remain silent. The decision to exercise that right cannot be considered or held against the defendant.

State that the government has the burden at trial to prove each and every element of the charges beyond a reasonable doubt. State that that burden is much higher than proof by preponderance of the evidence or "more likely than not," which is the standard in civil cases. Ask if anyone thinks that the government's burden of proof—beyond a reasonable doubt—is too high a standard or an unfair standard.

If particular issues arise based on the specific charges, discuss the possibility during jury selection. For instance, one issue that may arise in a securities fraud case is whether defendants acted in good faith. Explain good faith to the jurors. Also, explain that good faith is a complete defense to the charges of securities fraud and wire fraud. The essence of a good faith defense is that one who acts with honest intentions cannot be convicted of a crime requiring fraudulent intent. Ask whether anyone will have a problem finding that one or more of the defendants acted in good faith if the evidence warrants such a conclusion. Finally, ask if anyone would hesitate to vote "not guilty" if the government failed to prove its case.

Conducting Voir Dire

When asking questions, be sure to incorporate your case theory and theme. But please be mindful that opposing counsel may lodge an objection that counsel is attempting to try the case during jury selection. or the judge may raise the issue *sua sponte*. Make sure that you are taking meticulous notes and that another person on your team is doing likewise. Place stars on your list by your ideal jurors and an "x" by each juror who has talked themselves off the panel. Do not rush through the process. Take the time needed to do a thorough examination. Listen carefully to all the responses. Make a record of what is happening in the courtroom.

Striking Potential Jurors

When striking jurors, no counsel should exclude anyone based solely on race. The use of peremptory strikes to exclude a juror based solely on race is prohibited by the Equal Protection Clause of the Fourteenth Amendment. See *Batson v. Kentucky*, 476 U.S. 79 (1986). If counsel suspects opposing counsel has excluded a juror for racial reasons, counsel should issue a *Batson* challenge, which will trigger the court to conduct a three-part test. First, counsel must make a prima facie showing of racial discrimination that the prospective juror is a racial minority and that the individual was stricken because of race. Second, if such a showing is made, the burden shifts to opposing counsel to show that a racially neutral reason exists for striking the potential juror. Third, the court must determine whether counsel has proffered a race-neutral explanation or whether the reason given was pretextual.

3
Opening Statement

My favorite part of trial is the opening statement.

What the Evidence Will Show

Chief Justice Charles Evans Hughes noted that the "opening statement of counsel is ordinarily intended to do no more than to inform the jury in a general way of the nature of the action and defense so that they may better be prepared to understand the evidence."[1] An opening statement cannot be an argument or a detailed discussion of anticipated jury instructions or existing case law. Rather, counsel should tell the jury what the evidence will show and give a timeline of key events to give jurors a glimpse of what's to come. In short, your opening statement is a *statement*, not an argument, of what you believe the evidence will show. In a criminal case, the prosecutor delivers their statement first, followed by the statement by defense counsel. A great opening statement from the prosecutor's perspective must explain what trial counsel intends to prove and what witnesses and exhibits will help counsel prove such facts. The prosecutor should embrace the burden of proof and describe how the government will

[1] *Best v. District of Columbia*, 291 U.S. 411, 415 (1934).

meet its burden to prove the defendant guilty beyond a reasonable doubt, summarizing the facts of the case, using demonstrative aids and preadmitted exhibits if permitted by the court. The statement must be delivered within the time limits set by the court, typically 30 minutes.

A criminal defense lawyer should use the opening statement to humanize or personalize the defendant and explain that the allegations are simply untrue. It is best to discuss the defendant's background, family life, and work history. If the defendant does not have a clean record, admit in the opening that the defendant is not a Boy Scout or an angel. Discuss some of the shortcomings and then state that, nevertheless, the defendant did not do what is charged in the case. Highlight the positive aspects of the defendant. Has the defendant been raising their children by themselves? Did they become an informant for the government after being around the wrong people? Has the defendant been able to kick a drug habit? Is there evidence that the defendant is trying to leave the past behind them? Defense counsel should use an analogy to help explain reasonable doubt. Counsel may wish to emphasize that the government's burden is merely to tip the scale of justice beyond 50–50 and that the government must tip the scale all the way to the floor to meet their burden of proof beyond a reasonable doubt.

In a civil case, plaintiff's attorney goes first, followed by defense counsel. Both counsel should state what the evidence will show, giving a timeline of events and a preview of witnesses and key exhibits in chronological order. The presentations should be well organized, easy to follow, and straightforward. Counsel should discuss the burden of proof, which is a preponderance of the evidence, or just over 50 percent. Counsel should state that it will be up to the jury, the judges of the facts, to decide whether certain facts have been proven and are more likely true than not true. It is important to let jurors know that the burden of beyond a reasonable doubt is a stricter standard than more likely true than not true. Beyond a reasonable doubt is applicable in criminal cases, not in civil cases, and it should be put out of the jurors' minds. Use an analogy to help explain preponderance, for example: "The scale of justice is balanced 50–50 at the beginning of this trial. You must decide for the party that tips the scale to their favor with testimony and other evidence."

Write Your Opening Statement Word-for-Word

It is best to write out your opening statement word-for-word and to commit it to memory. Memorizing gives you the ability to maintain good eye contact with members of the jury. Some lawyers prefer to outline the opening and be flexible in the actual words that are uttered. While really experienced orators may be able to operate in that manner, the vast majority of us should be scripted, without sounding or acting scripted.

Keep revising your opening statement until it is exactly as you want it and fits with the time constraint the court has announced. Your opening statement may go through dozens of edits and revisions. It is very important to seek input from others to make the statement stronger. You may want to consider using a hook in the introduction. A hook is a sentence or phrase in the introduction that serves as an attention-grabber. Its effectiveness is defined by its capability to motivate the jury to listen more carefully. The hook should arouse interest but not be argumentative.

Remember that the opening is all about storytelling. Your story should paint a vibrant picture of the case. Be sure to use the active voice and language that reinforces your themes.

Should You Use Notes?

It is okay to have your written opening statement, or notes, at the podium or counsel's table, but you must not read your statement or notes to the jury. An overreliance on the statement or notes may signal to the jury that you do not understand the case as well as your opposing counsel does. If you are looking down too much, you also miss the opportunity to build rapport with the jurors.

The Introduction

Even if you were introduced to the jury during voir dire, it makes sense to introduce yourself again, as well as your co-counsel, when beginning your opening statement. A straightforward introduction is best. "May it please the court, ladies and gentlemen of the jury, my name is (full name). Along with my co-counsel (full name), we represent the government/defendant in this case."

How to Incorporate Case Theory and Theme

It is important to include your case theory and theme throughout the jury trial but especially in your opening and closing. Weave your theory and theme into your trial narrative. Your theory of the case is your elevator pitch. One or two sentences will tell the jury what your case is about. Johnnie Cochran once told a Los Angeles jury in an infamous murder case, albeit in closing, "If it doesn't fit, you have to acquit." In a drug case, a defense counsel may argue that John Doe was a meth user but never distributed the drug as charged: "Meth user, not a drug dealer." In a civil case, plaintiff's counsel may state, "My client, Jane Smith, was fired for blowing the whistle on an illegal activity to her employer, Giant Corporation LLC." Defense counsel may counter, "Plaintiff Jane Smith was lawfully terminated by Giant Corporation LLC for poor job performance, insubordination, missing key meetings, and being late for work on more than 20 occasions in the last calendar year."

How to Connect with Jurors

Maintain good eye contact and speak slowly and concisely. Once you have made a few statements, step away from the podium if the judge allows it. Use body language and voice to emphasize your most important points. Tell the jury why they are in the courthouse. For example, in a drug case state: "John Doe is charged with conspiracy to distribute 500 grams or more of a detectable substance containing methamphetamine." Or in an employment matter: "This case is brought under Missouri's antiretaliation whistle blower law, which prohibits an employer from retaliating against any employee who has a reasonable belief that an illegal activity has occurred and reported it."

Next, give the jury an overview of what you believe the evidence will show, presented from your client's perspective. The statement should be at the 30,000-foot level, avoiding being in the weeds. "The facts of this case are simple. The evidence will show that on July 17, 2017, John Doe first sold methamphetamine to an undercover DEA agent and a confidential informant."

Then give a brief explanation of what has to be proven. For example, in a drug trafficking case, the government has the burden and it never shifts to the defendant. "Under federal law, the government must prove the defendant violated three elements. First, we must prove the defendant possessed the controlled substance. Second, that he had knowledge that the controlled substance was being possessed illegally. Third, that the controlled substance was possessed for the purpose of a sale."

Give the jury a sneak peek at those witnesses who will be testifying at trial. "We will call four witnesses: Sarah Joe, Saul Brown, Michael Slater, and the case agent, Tim Jones."

Discuss the key testimony of each witness. "Ms. Sarah Joe will tell you that. . . . Next, the government will call Mr. Saul Brown, a co-defendant who will testify that . . . Michael Slater, an informant, will be able to describe for you how the defendant . . . And finally, FBI Agent Tim Jones will describe. . . ."

In a civil case, each party has the burden of proof. "This is a civil case and Plaintiff TJK Companies must prove his case by a preponderance of the evidence that. . . ." Explain briefly and demonstrate with your hands or the scales of justice what a preponderance of the evidence means.

Restate the theory of the case. "Missouri's product liability law exists to protect all of us from defective goods and to mandate that auto manufacturers produce safe cars. Defendant Automaker was negligent when it produced the Maincar with airbags that failed to deploy in the crash."

Tell the jury what you want. "For these reasons, after you have listened to and viewed all the evidence, at the end of this trial we will ask you to return a verdict in favor of the Plaintiff."

The same goes for a criminal case. "At the end of the trial, the United States will ask you to find the Defendant guilty of. . . ." Or "Based on the evidence you will hear, at the end of the trial the Defendant will ask you to return a verdict of not guilty."

Should You Use Exhibits?

If exhibits have been preadmitted by the parties, it can be quite effective to display those exhibits during your opening.

Should You Use a Timeline?

A timeline is a demonstrative exhibit that can help jurors follow your suggested timeline. It is best to show the timeline to opposing counsel and the court before displaying it to the jury. This issue can be taken up at the pretrial conference days before trial or on the day opening statements are to be given.

Should You Discuss Anticipated Witnesses?

It is important for jurors to know about anticipated witnesses, so mention the best ones who support your case theory and theme. FBI Agent Smith will testify . . . An expert witness will testify that. . . .

Mistakes to Avoid

Do not read your opening statement.

Do not argue during your opening statement. Save your argument for the closing argument.

Do not talk longer than the allotted time or the judge will stop you during your presentation.

Do not fail to mention the burden of proof.

Do not forget to request a verdict. Tell the jury exactly what you need it to do. In a criminal case that you are prosecuting, you need to ask the jury to return a verdict of guilty on all counts. If you are defending in a case, you need to request a verdict of not guilty on all counts. In a civil case, you need to request a verdict in your client's favor and a specific monetary award if appropriate.

Do not ask questions during opening statements. (Doing so will allow the jury to come up with answers you or your client may not want.)

Do not spend time on unimportant things or go deep into details, as jurors may lose focus.

Do not use too much legal jargon.

Performance and Style

It has been said that if you fail to prepare, you prepare to fail. So it is best to practice, practice, practice. You will never get a second chance to make that first impression on the jury. Be conscious of your areas of focus and energy. In addition to memorizing the content of your opening, memorize your movement, gestures, and points of emphasis. That is, use body posture and movement deliberately and consciously.

4
Trial Evidence

To win at trial, it comes down to evidence. The best advocates present evidence in a storytelling manner.

On Direct Examination:

1. Write out your questions word-for-word and don't be afraid to read. No one in the courtroom should be focused on you. The witness is the star on direct examination.
   However, be as familiar as possible with your questions so that you can watch the witness and listen to the answers. Witnesses sometimes do distracting things while testifying.
   For example, don't look around the courtroom, which can detract from their credibility.
2. Make sure your questions are nonleading. Leading questions are for cross examination; they will draw objections from opposing counsel. Opposing counsel may be able to make you look incompetent to members of the jury.
3. Write the anticipated answer below each question. Place a check mark by the answer once the witness testifies to that fact. This is a good way of making sure you are meeting the elements. I recommend counsel have a list of elements (especially in criminal cases) that they can check off as each element is established. A checklist prevents you from accidentally skipping a step.

4. Listen to the answers being given. Don't jump ahead thinking of your next question. It is amazing how many lawyers miss the answers they solicit by not paying attention.
5. Incorporate your case theory and theme into the questions you ask. Your witness is there to tell a story. Help weave the story together with open-ended questions that track how you think about the case.
6. Ask the important and essential questions, and then sit down. Too often I see counsel ask questions that don't help. The jury determines what the facts are.
7. Have a gameplan for getting documents into evidence through each witness. Make sure you march through all the right steps:

   I am showing you what has been marked as Exhibit 248 for identification purposes.
   Do you recognize this?
   What is it?
   How do you know?
   Is this a fair and accurate depiction?
   Your Honor, I move to admit Exhibit 248 into evidence.

8. Be prepared to respond to objections. The most common objections include leading, irrelevant, narrative speculation and hearsay. Keep a list of objections and responses at counsel's table. Know the statements that are not hearsay, including witnesses' prior statements and opposing party's statement. Know hearsay exceptions, which include reputation, public records, excited utterance, recorded recollection, and present sense impression.

On Cross Examination:

1. Identify a few broad areas you want to explore with the witness. Ask all leading questions. You do not want to open yourself up to some type of narrative. That witness gets to tell their side of the story on direct examination. You, the lawyer, are testifying on cross examination. Everyone should be looking at you. You are the star. Do not read from your notes.

2. If the witness does not answer your question, ask it again. If the witness fails to respond properly after you have asked the same question again, ask: "Is that a yes?" or "Is that a no?"
3. It is okay to fall; you just have to get back up. Sometimes a witness will get the best of you on cross examination. Take a deep breath and try again. Do not show the jury you've been hurt. You can switch to a different area if the examination is not going well.

More generally:

1. Keep track of exhibits admitted and time/day the document was admitted. Do not rely on the court to do your job.
2. Be respectful of all witnesses. Jurors do not like nasty lawyers who take cheap shots.
3. Pay attention when the court reads the jury instructions to the jurors. Mistakes sometimes happen. Protect the record and make sure the jury is instructed properly.

5
After the Close of All Evidence

Move for Judgment as a Matter of Law

Before the case proceeds to the jury, counsel should move for a judgment as a matter of law. If the court determines that a jury would not have a legally adequate evidentiary basis to find for a party, the court may resolve the issue against the party or dismiss the claim.

What the Evidence Shows

My second favorite part of any trial is the closing argument. A closing argument is counsel's attempt to frame for the jury what the evidence shows, after all witnesses have testified and document exhibits have been admitted. Counsel should remind the jury of the key evidence presented and show a timeline of crucial events to convince jurors of what has transpired. In short, your closing argument is an argument, not a statement, of what you believe the evidence admitted during trial confirms. In a criminal case, the prosecutor delivers their closing first, followed by defense counsel, and then a brief rebuttal by the government. A great closing argument from the prosecutor's perspective must explain what trial counsel proved and what witnesses and exhibits help show that counsel proved such facts. The prosecutor should embrace the burden of proof and describe how the government met its burden of proving the defendant guilty beyond a reasonable doubt, summarizing the facts of the case, and using demonstrative aids and admitted exhibits. The argument must be delivered within the time limits set by the court, which is typically 30 minutes.

A criminal defense lawyer should use the closing argument to further humanize or personalize the defendant and explain that the allegations were not proven beyond a reasonable doubt. It is best to argue that this case should never have come to trial, that the government has not produced one shred of evidence that the crime the defendant is charged with ever took place. Defense counsel may argue that the government has instead relied on the testimony of witnesses whose testimony was called into serious question upon cross examination. Defense counsel may also argue that if circumstantial evidence exists, it falls short of proving guilt beyond a reasonable doubt. Also, if the evidence on any element of a criminal offense is weak, or, according to the defendant, unproven, the defense should point this out clearly. Jurors should be reminded that, ultimately, it is up to each one of them to determine what facts are most important and that they are empowered to do justice, to ensure that America's great system of justice works.

In a civil case, plaintiff's attorney goes first, followed by defense counsel and then a brief rebuttal by plaintiff's counsel. Both counsel should argue what the evidence shows, giving a timeline of events and recapping witness testimony and key exhibits in chronological order. The presentations should be well organized, easy to follow, and straightforward. Counsel should discuss the burden of proof, which is a preponderance of the evidence, or just over 50 percent. Counsel should argue that it is now up to the jury to decide whether certain facts have been proven and whether certain facts are more likely true than not. And counsel should make frequent and specific reference to the evidence admitted during the course of the trial. In closing, it is important to let jurors know that the burden of beyond a reasonable doubt is a stricter standard than more likely true than not true. As noted earlier, beyond a reasonable doubt is applicable in criminal cases, not in civil cases, and should be put out of their minds. Use an analogy to help argue preponderance. "The scales of justice are balanced 50–50 at the beginning of this trial. You must decide for the party that tips the scales to their favor with testimony and other evidence. We did just that in this trial."

Write Your Closing Argument Word-for-Word

It is best to write out your closing argument word-for-word and commit it to memory. Memorizing gives you the ability to maintain good eye contact with members of the jury. Some lawyers prefer to outline the closing and stay flexible on the actual words that are uttered. Although really experienced orators may be able to operate in that manner, the vast majority of us should be scripted, without sounding or acting scripted.

Keep revising your closing argument until it is exactly as you want it and fits with the time constraint the court has announced. Your closing may go through dozens of edits and revisions. It is so important to seek input from others to make your argument stronger. As discussed earlier, you may want to consider a hook in the introduction, that is, a sentence or phrase that will serve as an attention-grabber. The effectiveness of the hook is defined by its capability to motivate the jury to listen more carefully. The hook should arouse interest and should be argumentative.

Remember that the closing, like the opening, is all about storytelling. Your story should paint a vibrant picture of the case and the evidence that jurors just heard and saw. Be sure to use an active voice and language that reinforces your themes. Jurors value consistency. The more your closing matches the promises made in the opening, the better.

Should You Use Notes?

It is preferable to have your written closing argument, or notes, at the podium or counsel's table, but you must not read your closing or notes to the jury. An overreliance on the written argument or notes may signal to the jury that you do not understand the case as well as your opposing counsel does. You also miss the opportunity to continue to build rapport with eye contact if you are looking down too much. If you are unable to memorize, do not fret. Many talented attorneys find memorization burdensome and unrealistic. At a minimum, counsel should argue from a short set of bullet points.

The Introduction

Even if you were introduced to the jury during voir dire and introduced yourself again during the opening statement, it makes sense to introduce yourself again, and co-counsel, when beginning your closing argument. A straightforward introduction is best. "May it please the court, ladies and gentlemen of the jury, my name is (full name). Along with my co-counsel (full name), it has been a pleasure to represent the government/defendant in this case."

How to Incorporate Case Theory and Theme

It is important to include your case theory and theme throughout the jury trial but especially in the closing argument. Weave your theory and theme into your trial summation. As a reminder, your theory of the case is your elevator pitch. These one or two sentences tell the jury what your case is about. Remember the example I gave earlier from Johnnie Cochran's closing in the O. J. Simpson trial: "If it doesn't fit, you have to acquit." In a drug case, a defense counsel may argue that John Doe was a meth user, but never distributed the drug as charged: "Meth user, not a drug dealer." In a civil case, plaintiff's counsel may argue, "My client, Jane Smith, was fired for blowing the whistle on an illegal activity to her employer, Giant Corporation LLC." Defense counsel may counter with: "Plaintiff Jane Smith was lawfully terminated by Giant Corporation LLC for poor job performance, insubordination, missing key meetings, and being late for work on more than 20 occasions in the last calendar year."

How to Connect with Jurors

Maintain good eye contact and speak slowly and concisely. Once you have made a few arguments, step away from the podium if the judge allows it. Use your body language and voice to emphasize your most important points. Tell the jury why they have been in the courthouse for days (or weeks). In a drug case, "John Doe was charged with conspiracy to distribute 500 grams or more of a detectable substance containing methamphetamine." In an employment matter, "This case was brought under Missouri's antiretaliation whistleblower law, which prohibits an employer from retaliating against any employee who has a reasonable belief that an illegal activity has occurred and reported it."

Next, give the jury an overview of what you contend the evidence showed at trial, presented from your client's perspective. The argument should be at the 10,000-foot level, with counsel getting into the weeds. "The facts of this case are simple. The evidence clearly shows that on July 17, 2017, John Doe first sold methamphetamine to an undercover DEA agent and a confidential informant."

Then give a brief explanation of what has been proven. For example, in a drug trafficking case, the government has the burden, and it never shifts to the defendant. "Under federal law, the government must prove, and has proved, all three elements of the crime. First, we proved that the defendant possessed the controlled substance. Second, that he had knowledge that the controlled substance was being possessed illegally. Third, that the controlled substance was possessed for the purpose of a sale."

Give the jury a recap of the witnesses who have testified at trial. "We called four witnesses: Sarah Joe, Saul Brown, Michael Slater, and the case agent, Tim Jones."

Discuss the key testimony of each witness. "Ms. Sarah Joe told you that. . . . Next, the government called Mr. Saul Brown, a codefendant who testified that. . . . Michael Slater, an informant, described for you how the defendant. . . . And finally, FBI Agent Tim Jones described. . . . " It is quite effective to argue, "I told you this when we started and you heard witnesses say that very thing." Along the same lines, counsel should note what opposing counsel says in their opening. If they make promises or forecasts but do not keep them, counsel can pound the opposition with those lapses in closing.

In a civil case, each party has the burden of proof. "This is a civil case and Plaintiff TJK Companies must prove his case by a preponderance of the evidence that. . . ." Explain briefly and demonstrate with your hands or the scales of justice what a preponderance of the evidence means.

Restate the theory of the case. "Missouri's product liability law exists to protect all of us from defective goods, and to mandate that auto manufacturers produce safe cars. Defendant Automaker was negligent when it produced the Maincar with airbags that failed to deploy in the crash."

Tell the jury what you want. "For these reasons, after you have discussed, reviewed, and analyzed all the evidence, we will ask you to return a verdict in favor of the Plaintiff."

The same goes for a criminal case. "Now that we have come to the end of the trial the United States asks you to find the Defendant guilty of. . . . " Or "Based on the evidence you have heard, and now that we are at the end of the trial, the Defendant asks you to return a verdict of not guilty."

Should You Use Exhibits?

If exhibits have been admitted during trial, it can be quite effective to display them during your closing argument.

Should You Use a Timeline?

A timeline is a demonstrative exhibit that can help jurors follow your case theme and theory. It is best to show the timeline to opposing counsel and the court before displaying it to the jury in closing. This issue can be taken up on the day closing arguments are to be given. It makes the most sense to use the same timeline from opening statements if you have proven what is depicted there.

Should You Discuss Witness Testimony?

The answer is most definitely. It is important for jurors to know what you think about the testimony of important witnesses, so mention the best ones who support your case theory and theme. FBI Agent Smith testified. . . . An expert witness, Dr. Smith, testified that. . . . Nevertheless, I caution you about stating "I believe" because counsel is not permitted to assert a personal opinion about the evidence in any case.

Mistakes to Avoid

Do not read your closing argument.

Do not deliver your closing argument in a neutral, dispassionate manner. The closing argument is very different from the opening statement.

Do not talk longer than the allotted time or the judge will stop you during your presentation.

Do not fail to argue the burden of proof.

Do not forget to request a verdict. Tell the jury exactly what you need it to do. In a criminal case that you are prosecuting, you need to ask the jury to return a verdict of guilty on all counts. If you are defending, you need to request a verdict of not guilty on all counts. In a civil case, you need to request a verdict in your client's favor and a specific monetary award if appropriate.

Do ask questions during the closing argument (it allows the jury to come up with answers instead of you doing the hard work for them).

Do not spend time on unimportant things or go deep into details as jurors may lose focus.

Do not use too much legal jargon.

If opposing counsel makes an improper closing argument, do object or the issue may be waived on appeal.

Do not make emotionally laden statements that inflame the passions of the jury.

Performance and Style

It has been said that if you fail to prepare, you prepare to fail. So it is best to practice, practice, practice. Be conscious of your areas of focus and energy. In addition to memorizing the content of your closing, memorize your movement, gestures, and points of emphasis. That is, use body posture and movement deliberately and consciously.

Should You Poll the Jurors?

If you get an adverse jury verdict, it is wise to poll the jury. Once requested, the judge will give each juror the chance, before the verdict is logged, to declare in open court their concurrence with the verdict.

The court will make sure that the verdict has in fact been reached and that no juror has been pressured or forced to agree to a verdict to which they have not fully agreed. If polling discloses lack of consensus by a juror, the court may instruct the jury to continue to deliberate or order a new trial.

Should You Talk with Jurors Afterward?

Win or lose, if the court will allow, you should talk with the jurors following trial. You should ask what they thought of your trial presentation, the various witnesses, and the parties.

Does Your Client Want to Appeal?

Find out how your client would like to proceed. Document in writing how the client has instructed you to proceed and then follow instructions.

Part II
Trial Lawyer Interviews

The remaining chapters in this book present transcripts of several interviews I conducted of four extremely talented trial lawyers. The interviews were conducted over several months during the fall and winter of 2022, via telephone, email, or both. None of these lawyers has ever appeared before me sitting as a trial judge. All counsel are on my recusal list. I am so very grateful for their time and participation.

6

Lori G. Cohen

Partner, Greenberg Traurig, Atlanta

Lori Cohen first came across my radar screen in 2009 or 2010 when I practiced product liability defense at Shook, Hardy & Bacon, representing automotive clients such as Ford Motor Company and pharmaceutical giants such as Eli Lilly & Company. Lori, an Atlanta-based trial lawyer, stood out to me because she had a trial record of 46–0 in 2009, and not surprisingly, enjoyed a rock star reputation. I could not intellectually process such a pristine record for someone in private practice. Sure, I knew federal prosecutors who had run the tables, only taking slam dunk cases to trial. But I had never met a private practitioner in such a sophisticated practice area who was undefeated at trial. Was Lori as good and dominant as the 1972 Dolphins who went 17–0, defeated the Washington Redskins, 14–7, in Super Bowl VII, and became the first and only NFL team to complete a perfect undefeated season?

A decade later, Lori is now Vice Chair of Greenberg Traurig (GT) and serves as Co-Chair of the firm's Global Litigation Practice, leading a group of over 600 attorneys nationally and internationally. She is Co-Chair of the Trial Practice Group, her "brainchild," which she created at GT. Upon joining GT, she also built the Pharmaceutical,

Medical Device and Health Care Litigation Practice. Under her leadership, this practice grew to include over 100 attorneys in more than 30 offices in the United States and globally; in 2018, the group was named the *American Lawyers*' "Product Liability Litigation Department of the Year." Most recently, *Law360* has recognized Lori and her team as "Product Liability Group of the Year" in both 2021 and 2022.

Nationally recognized for her extraordinary trial record of 58 defense verdicts in 2022, Lori leads a global practice that focuses on product liability, pharmaceutical, medical device, and health care litigation. She has served as national, regional, and trial counsel for numerous medical device and pharmaceutical manufacturers, handling all types of litigation, including class actions, multidistrict litigation, and trials nationally. Lori and her team routinely take complex cases to trial and win, including some of the most complex mass torts in history. Well known for her ability to win high-stakes trials, she is often called upon to "parachute in" at the last minute before trial, especially in challenging cases in dangerous jurisdictions.

Lori has been described as a high-energy, high-profile leader among trial attorneys and is also acclaimed as an effective, passionate mentor. In an industry where two-thirds of all attorneys in civil cases are men and women represent only a quarter of lead or trial counsel, Lori stands out as a leader, who happens to be a woman, and a champion of developing the next generation of attorneys, particularly diverse attorneys. She is widely regarded for her ability to build strong, diverse, trial-ready teams made up of not just lawyers but nurses, in-house graphics/demonstrative designers, technology consultants, paralegals, and legal assistants, who are "all hands on deck" up to and through trial.

Lori has been profiled twice in "Winning Litigators," a special report in *The National Law Journal* that recognizes the top U.S. litigators. *The National Law Journal* also named her as one of "The 50 Most Influential Women Lawyers in America" and declared two of her defense trial victories "Top Defense Wins." Courtroom View Network recognized her team's victory in a pelvic mesh trial in state court in Missouri as the "Top Defense Verdict of 2016."

Lori is one of two attorneys listed in *The Legal 500*'s "Hall of Fame" for product liability litigation involving pharmaceutical and medical devices. She is also one of a very small group of attorneys selected nationally for inclusion in the 2010–2022 editions of *Chambers USA* Guide's National Pharmaceutical Industry Products Liability Table. Lori was named the 2019 "Product Liability Attorney of the Year" by *Benchmark Litigation* and has been selected as a "National Practice Area Star" (2020–2023), "Top 10 Women Litigator" (2018–2022), "Top 100 Trial Lawyer" (2018–2023), "Local Litigation Star" (2000–2023), and a "National Litigation Star" (2019). Lori is also listed in *The Best Lawyers in America*, *Chambers USA* Guide, *Chambers Global* Guide, *Outstanding Lawyers in America*, the *International Who's Who of Business Lawyers*, *The International Who's Who of Life Science Lawyers*, *The International Who's Who of Products Liability Defense Lawyers*, and *Georgia Super Lawyers* magazine.

She has served as an instructor for the National Institute for Trial Advocacy (NITA) and the Emory Law School Trial Techniques Program, and she has served as a faculty member of the International Association of Defense Council's (IADC) elite Trial Academy. I interviewed her on December 2, 2022.

Willie J. Epps Jr. (WJE): You made your name focusing on product liability litigation and specifically, medical device and pharmaceutical litigation, and you just obtained your 58th defense verdict at trial. Did you always want to be a trial lawyer growing up?

Lori G. Cohen (LGC): Yes, I absolutely always wanted to be a trial lawyer growing up, and as I look back on things, I am not sure exactly how or where that started. As far back as I can remember, I liked advocacy whether at home, much to the chagrin of my family, or in fourth grade when I decided to start a petition to get one of my teachers a better benefits/salary package that would cause him to stay at my grammar school. But I did not have any lawyers in my family, never mind any trial lawyers. I was enthralled by watching lawyers on TV, and in the movies and as things progressed, I became even more enthralled by the trial lawyers I was lucky enough to see in person in court too.

WJE: I understand your father had a huge influence on your life, even though he was not a lawyer or a professional. Is he the one who planted big dreams into you as a young girl, and did he encourage you to pursue a legal career?

LGC: I had a very special relationship with my dad, who taught me that I could do anything and to never take no for an answer. He was a blue-collar worker and only found himself dealing with attorneys or courthouses when he had the occasional speeding ticket or when he ended up in small claims court over a squabble with a customer. He would always represent himself and always fight whatever alleged injustice he felt had happened. He encouraged this public school kid from a town south of Boston to go the distance in whatever I chose to do and when I did not apply timely to Duke University but regretted it later, he called up Duke admissions somehow and found someone to agree to accept my application late. He explained that I would not let them down if given the chance. That one call by this humble yet strong man, my dad, would change my life forever and my destiny for sure. The other lesson he taught me was to always outwork everyone else to gain the advantage, and that became part of my brand; I came by that naturally, since he worked until he was 86.

WJE: I read that you grew up wanting to be a female Atticus Finch, the fictional character in Harper Lee's *To Kill a Mockingbird*, which is one of my all-time favorite books and a really good movie. Finch defends a Black man at trial who is accused in the 1930s of raping a young white woman in the Deep South. Finch knew his way around that Alabama courtroom and, despite the adverse verdict, did all he could to get his client acquitted. As you know, it is not easy for lawyers to get into a courtroom to master the art of trial advocacy. How did you first access the courtroom to gain experience?

LGC: I absolutely love that book and that movie, and my husband has lost count of how many times he has found me glued to the screen watching it again and again. With Atticus in the back of my mind and after starting at the law firm of Alston & Bird in Atlanta in 1990, I made it my mission to get into trial as early and as often as possible no matter what it took, harkening back to my dad's lessons to me. As a young associate, I had my assignments and assigned attorneys to whom I was obligated. Beyond that, I quickly found out who in the firm went to trial the most and embarked on getting to know them and making myself indispensable to them while making sure I kept up my other commitments. I promised those attorneys, really three wonderful mentors for me, that if they would just let me help on their trials, I would do it in my free time, i.e., nights, weekends, whenever. I realized that the medical malpractice group had the most trials and had the need for a young, eager, female associate to roll up her sleeves. That start is what then catapulted me into court mostly alongside and against much older male attorneys. In the early 1990s, it was unusual to find a young woman trying very serious medical cases, and the clients, judges, and every opposing counsel seemed to like it. I was starting a new trend, but I did not see many other women in the courtroom, especially as lead trial counsel, or taking a serious role in the trials, for many years to come. But I used it to my advantage and connected with female jurors and female judges and expert witnesses. Practicing in the South primarily in the early years, I did have a few run-ins with judges who called me "honey" or "sweetie" and like others in my day, had the typical "are you the court reporter" inquiry, but I never minded, and I preferred to let everyone underestimate me until it was too late and victory was in my sights, making my clients very happy.

WJE: You have had an incredible work ethic your entire life, growing up in South Boston, doing work study during college and law school, waiting tables at Shenanigan's Restaurant. Leveraging your life experiences, what are three things you did to become a top trial lawyer?

LGC: That is a great question and one I have never been asked exactly that way. First, I would say always outwork the opposition or be willing to work as hard and as much as necessary. Never be afraid of hard work or no sleep or giving it your all no matter what it takes. Second, but not necessarily less important than the first answer, is to stay true to yourself and thus be able to connect with anyone from any walk of life. This is another thing that came from my dad who would literally talk to everyone on a street in Atlanta or an elevator in a hotel. But as a trial lawyer you must be both credible and likeable. The jurors can see through any act, any airs, any façade, and any attempt at being someone you are not. I want jurors to believe me and trust that what is coming out of my mouth is true, albeit sprinkled with the necessary advocacy of course! I can harken back to all the people I communicated with in my fast-food, waitressing, and bartending days.

I like to say that everything I learned about lawyering and talking to jurors emanates from my days at Wendy's, Burger King, McDonald's, and Shenanigan's, to name some of my prior employers. Third, given the high-profile and serious damages cases I try and handle, I think it is very important to always remain empathetic to the plaintiff and never lose sight of their plight. To do so would be a mistake. Some of the plaintiffs have suffered unimaginable losses, family members, and even their own future. I remember attending the funeral of one of my plaintiffs who died of ovarian cancer and how much it meant to her family. I also remember a case I had in Georgia in the late 1990s with a very young mother whose baby had suffered devastating brain injuries at or before birth. She and I were the only women in the court every day, and we bonded, even though I was the opposing counsel. She felt overlooked by her team of older male attorneys, and with their permission, I stayed in touch with her after both lengthy trials of her case and I met her to try and explain things from the defense perspective, so she had a better understanding of what happened to her beautiful little boy. Importantly, these things only happen by remaining empathetic, and again, this cannot be contrived but real and jurors can figure that out.

WJE: Top lawyers and general counsel know you today . . . but how were you treated decades ago when you were beginning your career? How difficult was it being a woman in a male-dominated profession?

LGC: I touched on this above already. But let me expand a bit here. There were certainly some instances of challenging experiences in those early years in the remote courthouses, especially in the deeper south than Atlanta. Judges could be tough on me or speak to my older mentors and partners and ignore me. But importantly, I never minded and instead used that to fuel my fire and spur me to fight harder, work harder, prove myself. Also, as soon as I showed up as lead counsel and took the reins, and they saw that I could hold my own, I thought it was an advantage ultimately. I was a bit of a novelty, you might say. I was oftentimes underestimated, and that was fun when I turned the tables on the other side or surprised the judge. I was also incredibly lucky because I had male mentors who never held me back and always supported me. Also, my clients, starting in the 90s, were very supportive and never made me take a back seat once I had earned my stripes. I remember once in 1994 when I explained to my mentors that I had been invited to present on how I tried a case to a large group of outside counsel and a medical device in-house team. They assumed they or one of them would go with me. I told them the invitation was to me, I had created the opportunity, and if they went, I would forever be the junior member of the team, which I did not want. They ultimately understood and stayed home! I went alone, and it opened the doors to my 30 years of medical device litigation work.

WJE: Clients have called you a "Trial Wizard" who uses creative approaches to explain to lay jurors complex evidence. In addition, you are known to use technology in courtroom presentations of complex medical, scientific, and other catastrophic injury cases. Explain how you do what you do. And what are three things a lawyer can do to win a federal jury trial?

LGC: I absolutely love to create drama and storytelling in the courtroom and bring everything to life in a way that captivates and captures the attention of the jury. No one likes a boring trial that is black and white only. I try to bring color and keep the jurors' rapt attention. In addition to earning their trust by being credible, I too earn their gratitude by teaching them the medicine, the science, and the evidence in interesting and even multimedia ways. My secret weapon is my amazing trial graphics specialist who works side by side with me on my case and ultimately my trials. Gerard Buitrago has been working with me for decades; since I left my prior firm and moved to Greenberg Traurig. I do not hire a company or have others do things like animations and graphics for me. That is too impersonal and sterile to me. Most of the demonstratives we use at trial are from my imagination and working side by side with Gerard. He is part of our team, knows our clients, knows our experts, knows our witnesses, knows our cases, and therefore is invaluable. Early on in my cases or pretrial preparation, I am dreaming about how to present my themes, my story, and all to a jury. I am constantly thinking about what will work best and have the most impact on the jury. I work closely with Gerard and my trial team on all such demonstratives, and I even test them out on laypeople. Colors matter, words matter, font matters . . . everything down to the periods or commas matter to me!

The three things I think are critical to do to win a trial are:

1. Figure out early what are the themes you want to present to the jury that will explain

why your side should win. I develop the themes that will tell our story and refute the other side's story.

2. Who are the witnesses—fact and expert and other evidence—who can support those themes and how; and
3. how do we then bring each theme to life? Which demonstratives? Which animations? Which pictures? Which diagrams?

I do not leave this to others to do, but rather we do this together, and I love teaching the team how to do this and the importance of doing this well, with creativity and passion!

WJE: How do you prepare and use a trial notebook?

LGC: Different attorneys prepare trial notebooks different ways, and they can serve different purposes depending on individual preference. In my early years, my trial notebook was large and had everything in it, including witness outlines. Over time, that became too bulky and not manageable size-wise for me. In the past decade, I transformed the trial notebook to contain the key documents I wanted at my fingertips, literally by my side in court. It became more of a medium-size binder this way and does not purport to contain everything. This includes for me: trial calendar; themes document; trial plan, key rulings, pretrial order, witness list, and things like that. It is a medium-size binder of whatever documents I like in hard copy and within my grasp in court. I do separate binders for witness information, whether it be for cross or direct. I also include key information about the judge and their requirements for trial.

WJE: How do you prepare and use a timeline?

LGC: Timelines are excellent and important trial tools and demonstratives. I usually have a medical timeline for the plaintiff's medical history, and oftentimes too I may have a regulatory timeline or a company story/key fact timeline related to the liability issues facing my client. I try to present a timeline in my opening to give an overview of the histories of the plaintiff and the liability issues separately. I use them too with witnesses, both fact and expert, depending on the timeline—for instance, the plaintiff. I will then come back to it at the end in closing. This way I can explain to the jury what they are going to see and learn. I can refer to it with plaintiff and other witnesses during trial and come back to it in the end to show them what they learned for a "we've come full circle" experience. My timelines tend to be detailed, thematic, and color-coded, and I try to tell a story and support my themes with my timelines. When I am putting together a timeline, I am thinking about how I will use it at trial, what themes it supports, what messages it conveys. For example, we might use a timeline to show that a plaintiff had many medical issues that long preceded her surgery, or a device or medication that is being alleged to have caused the harm. Alternatively, I might use a timeline to show how much a company client did to investigate a problem or to test a device or product and show in great detail all the many steps it took to make a well-designed and sound product through its diligence. The timelines must grab the jurors' attention and convey your themes and a direct message.

WJE: When do you first analyze the jury instructions for a case headed to trial?

LGC: Jury instructions are usually due either at the pretrial conference or at the start of trial. So, I am usually reviewing them and thinking about them before trial and in conjunction with the jury interrogatories and verdict form. In my view, these are all critically important, but the jury interrogatories and verdict form are especially important, as they will be the last thing the jurors see while deliberating and before rendering a verdict. They are also a work in progress, and you must go back to them during trial as claims might be dropped or changed. Usually, I have one "legal eagle" person on my team who is assigned the critical job of managing the jury instructions and the charge conference at trial. They can then really dig in and navigate and negotiate the intricacies of the law and scrutinize the other side's charges too. Admittedly, however, I am obsessed about verdict forms and jury interrogatories and worry about them incessantly. You must read them over and over again and make sure they are easy to understand, and you are not creating a confusing or inconsistent situation for jurors. This could have bad repercussions later for a verdict you want to maintain.

WJE: How early do you develop your case theory and case theme?

LGC: I think you should create your case theory and themes, as I call them, during the fact discovery period. You want to have a starting point for these that you will then massage during the course of discovery. They too are a breathing, living set of themes that will change out of necessity over time in the case. But I think that witnesses should be prepared based on the case themes. Experts should buy into and understand the themes; you should use your experts as well as fact witnesses to help develop themes. Everyone on the team should know and live by these case themes, and all depositions should track themes. This is critical for consistency and for powerfully creating a case that is driving these themes forward to tell your story effectively and strategically. They are dynamic in that they must change to adapt with the developing facts and evidence. However, I always say if you are working on and creating your themes for trial and not as part of the case, you have missed the boat on the effective use of themes! They are not an afterthought or something you must do, but rather the team, the witnesses, fact, and expert, should be living and breathing these themes. They are the building blocks for a great trial that again uses and builds on these earlier themes.

WJE: How do you prepare your opening statement and closing argument, and when?

LGC: Again, I would start with the caveat that everyone prepares opening statements and closing arguments differently; it is a very personalized process for a lead trial attorney. You must find your style and your own "groove." They are also very different in how you prepare each, but I do try to link them together, as I will explain further.

For me, the opening statement is usually started weeks before trial starts but is modified, revised, and finessed up to the last moment at trial. But you should have a polished draft ready to go before you pack your bags and move to the trial site, so you are just tweaking it in the acute period leading up to trial. The opening will be your first real conversation with the jury and your first promises to them, i.e., where your credibility can be tested, and you must be sure of the promises you do make. In the early years, I focused much more on drafting an opening statement and would bolster it by picking and choosing which large poster boards and hard demonstrative evidence to show the jury during opening. In more recent years, since the early 2000s, my focus is on preparing the opening PowerPoint that I like to use and talk from to give my opening statement. I began using the opening PowerPoint long before it became in vogue to do so, and I think it became one of my trademarks for trials. I put a lot of personal blood, sweat, and tears into the opening PowerPoint, and I obsess over every word, every color, every illustration, and toil over it until I feel it is perfect and then I will go back and change it more, even throughout the opposing opening statement. Of course, how far you can go and how long you can speak turn on the rules of court of the particular judge and if you and opposing counsel have reached any agreement about the parameters of the opening. It is always best if you can reach agreement on things like the exchange of demonstratives to be shown to jury in opening to avoid last-minute battles on that first day when you want to be totally zen before speaking to the jury. Openings are where you set forth many things, but it is undoubtedly built around your themes, your story, and the evidence supporting all of that; at the same time, it is where you poke holes in the other side's case and show the forthcoming evidence that will refute what your adversary has just said. Regardless of all of your planning, you must be nimble on your toes and ready to pivot and address what your adversary dishes out in opening. Do not let any scurrilous comments be left standing or attacks unchallenged; look for ways to punch holes in them, but it takes the ability to counterattack on the spot. Be fearless!

Closings are a whole different ball of wax. This is what I like to call a walk down memory lane of the trial. Closing preparation starts during opening where you are noting the promises made by your opponent and hoping they do not keep them or fumble on what evidence they claim exists. You and your team must keep vigilant notes from that point forward in the trial and keep ongoing notes—"closing notes"—to pull from later when preparing the closing PowerPoint and argument. The closing argument PowerPoint and framework is built off your opening and what you said and then is strengthened with the evidence and testimony from trial, the meat to add to the bones. The closings will contain the best testimonial quotes, the best concessions, the best supportive evidence—the highlights of the trial in favor of your client. The key is finding and pulling together those jewels from trial in the most cohesive and impactful way.

Every trial attorney will tell you that the closing argument is the "crème de la crème" of trial, when you get to really strut your stuff and be your best advocate or Atticus (or both). Jurors also take closing very seriously (they may even dress up!) and know it is a big deal, and the case will be in their hands soon.

WJE: How do you approach direct examination and cross examination?

LGC: So much has been written and said about direct examinations and cross examinations at trial that I probably cannot do justice to the topics in a limited response, but I will try to give some of the key points as I see them. Plain and simple, direct examinations should go well for you, or you have done something poorly or have not prepared yourself or your witness well enough.

The hardest thing about direct examination is getting your witness ready for cross examination by the other side, and this should never—I repeat, never—be taken for granted. Get your witness ready and his direct examination will go well. Direct examination should be an easier part of trial, one that you can prepare far in advance and take the ensuing time to meet with your witness, whether it be fact or expert, and really make it something of beautiful artistry. It should flow, tell a story, carry forth your themes, and convince the jury of your side of the story while also enhancing the witnesses' credibility and likeability. You want the jury to think your witnesses, experts, and fact witnesses are smarter and, also, the man or woman you would want to sit with over a glass of wine, beer, or coffee to help explain the case to them in a kind and friendly (not condescending) way. Your direct examination should be the ultimate overprepared presentation that comes across as fluid and not scripted at all. The art is to prepare so much with your witness for direct that you can both enjoy the testimony and presentation to the jury and have it seem like a casual, yet informative, conversation to the jury. Also, of course, using the right and best (meaning most illustrative and theme-driven) demonstratives whether they be animations, models, devices, videos that will cause the jury to be leaning forward mouths agape in awe, excitement, and enthralled by the information you and your witness are sharing.

Cross examinations are much harder to prepare and to conduct well, but they are all the more satisfying when they are done well, and you score unanticipated points or even those that may be anticipated. Think of Atticus in his cross examination of Mayella Ewing establishing that her right eye was blackened, that Bob is left-handed, and that Tom's left arm is useless.

The art of a brilliant and successful cross examination is in the preparation. And if you think you have prepared enough, prepare some more. The job ahead of a cross examiner is to make sure that you know more about the person you are to cross examine than the witness knows. What do I mean by that? It is up to you to do what I call "scorched earth" investigation and find everything under the sun ever written or stated by the witness, whether in articles, resumes, websites, press, social media, blogs, court filings, criminal records, legal proceedings—you name it. You may not want to or even be allowed to use it all, but first you must unearth it and find all the potential jewels. The jewels are out there, and you and your team must do everything to find them and then organize them in the most compelling way for the great setup at trial. Preparing for cross examination is like peeling a big onion and peeling and peeling and peeling. Never stop until you have enough fodder to turn the witness inside out or upside down on the stand. Alternatively, if you have a witness whom you must be empathetic toward, you should make sure you have combed their medical records for information and prepare a kinder, gentler cross examination.

One of the most fertile grounds for cross examination fodder is in prior depositions, especially for adverse experts who are avid testifiers or, as we say, repeated offenders. I will often hear from my team that "there is nothing good out there" on this person. My common refrain is "yes there is"—"go back and keep looking." I have never failed to find some good cross examination fodder in prior testimony, but you must turn over every stone and be willing to hunt and hunt again and hunt some more. Then, you must figure out how to use to your advantage and in a way that convinces the jury that the witness is either not being honest, not worth believing, or will say anything depending on who hired them. By pulling out all of the stops and doing "scorched earth" investigations, you will unearth secrets on just about anyone, and, at a minimum, you will know exactly how they think and will testify to prepare for the trial face-down against them.

Also, always make sure to listen carefully at trial to the witness on direct. I like to say witnesses will always go too far on the stand and often contradict themselves or other witness or what their attorney or the one who retained them promised during opening statement. Jump on what they said during direct like a lion on prey. Be ready to pivot, and don't be scripted but jump on those moments and opportunities.

Last but not least, when you are putting your actual cross examination together, try to make it as punchy and hard-hitting as possible; try to have a certain number (four? six? eight?) of areas or themes of your cross, depending on the witness and the case. Also, have a topic that is very strong to start and always end on a high note, meaning a guaranteed crushing blow to the opposing witness! Start strong, end strong, keep it interesting, hold a tight leash, and you must do the leading and most of the speaking at all times of course! Do not let the opposing witness on cross take charge or assume the lead and grab the mike. Cross-exam time is the examiner's time to shine or should be, so always grab the mike back or simply do not let it go!

WJE: How many cases have you tried to verdict? How many in federal court? Civil and criminal?

LGC: I have tried 65 cases of all kinds—including pro bono cases—to verdict. About 10 of those were in federal court. None of them were criminal. Of those cases, as noted above, I had 58 defense verdicts. I had two that were hung juries. I had two that were plaintiffs' verdicts but relatively small verdicts; one of the cases was sent to us in default, and we tried only damages, and it was considered a "win" given how low the damages were. One was a plaintiff's significant verdict, including punitives, which was reversed by the court of appeals and is still currently on appeal.

WJE: Let's talk about your high-profile cases. Describe what you did to win. Please give details of any interesting trial moments.

LGC: As my years as a trial lawyer progressed, the cases became more and more high profile. I tried a number of pelvic or vaginal mesh cases which garnered significant attention, including one plaintiff's verdict, including punitives but limited damages, both compensatory and punitives; one verdict is the significant plaintiff's verdict that was overturned on appeal and is still on appeal; one verdict was a total defense verdict and had many exciting "Perry Mason" moments at trial. In that case in Missouri state court, downtown Kansas City, what really won the case for us was dismantling the plaintiff and her main medical expert and proving that they were both not credible by catching them in either major mistruths or errors if you want to be charitable in front of the jury. This was accomplished by the great work of my team who did an amazing job (1) finding great experts;

(2) finding "secret" medical records that had never been produced for us; (3) allowing me to set up both the plaintiff and her expert witness by committing to positions on the stand when they testified and even the opposing counsel being committed to a position in opening. During trial, my team never gave up and was vigilantly pursuing old records, through all means possible. even down to convincing a hospital in Texas to send an employee to an old shed to find microfiche that allowed us to prove the plaintiff, her expert, and even the attorney wrong in many dramatic moments in court and to elevate and bolster the credibility of our own expert, who had predicted exactly what these records would show, despite their existence being denied by the other side. This undoubtedly helped us achieve this verdict after an incredibly long trial and a holiday break in the middle.

In another high-profile case involving many defendants, and all of them pointing at my client to try to ensure we would end up on the verdict form and absorb an anticipated high verdict, we were able to avoid being on the verdict form at all with a very exciting defense verdict. We were the only corporate defendant in state court in Seattle, in a very tragic case with all other parties and counsel being the hometown teams but us.

The plaintiff had suffered an unimaginable injury called a "blowtorch injury" and was left on a ventilator for life unable to speak or breathe or function without this mechanical airway for her. Through our trial strategy (which I planned and started early in the case), we were able to position ourselves as the defendant that did not belong—as I asked of the jury in opening and also in closing repeatedly as my mantra, "why are we here?" There was significant strategy that started early in the case, in depositions and motions too, by always going last, always asking questions in a certain way, and finally at trial by our strategy, down to where we sat at the tables in the courtroom and what we even used as tables (a flimsy card table). Though our actions, our words, and our optics in front of the jury, as well as the testimony we had elicited carefully in discovery, we positioned ourselves as an "afterthought," who did not belong in this Seattle courtroom and was there as a "deep pocket" only with no concrete or clear evidence of liability. This approach worked in this case, but it only worked because I had masterminded this plan from the get-go in the case. I could envision how it would play out at trial years later, and thankfully, it worked, despite all the finger pointing at us and as I call it, the "circular firing squad." This is what I also call "beginning with the end in mind"—visualizing what your closing argument might be far off in the distance and thinking hard early on about how to effectuate that vision.

WJE: Please explain the different types of trial lawyers you have observed through the years. Which kinds are most effective in front of a jury?

LGC: Trial lawyers must be confident to stand in court and effectively represent one's client fully and effectively. There are certainly the loud, showy, bombastic attorneys who capture the court and jury attention early and quickly. There are the quiet, studious, more reserved types who earn the respect of the jury and judge over time by mastery of the law and fact. And there is everything in between. The most effective attorneys in front of the jury are the ones who stay true to themselves because anything else is just a facade which will fall apart in a trial. Also, ones who know the law, know the facts, know their client and the opposing party or parties like the back of their hand. Any attorney who comes to trial and is not prepared and just wants to 'wing it" because they may be talented will not ultimately keep the respect of a jury. A jury is smart and will be able to tell if the "emperor has no clothes." There is no substitute for over-preparation, especially if you are learning to become a great trial attorney. If you are going to trial or in trial and you are either not nervous or not trying to learn more about the case all the time, you are not pressuring yourself enough. You can and should be confident but never overconfident.

WJE: How do you deal with bad advice from co-counsel?

LGC: You may receive bad advice from your co-counsel or your local counsel or even your team and client sometimes. You should always consider it and pay attention to any advice; do not just brush it off or fail to acknowledge it, but ultimately you are responsible and must own and make the decision. Always be respectful and discuss the issue at hand, but then you must make the call if you are lead trial counsel.

WJE: What is the best way to develop into a top trial attorney?

LGC: The best way to develop into a top trial attorney is to really want it, to dream it, and to visualize it. You must absolutely love it and want it badly, as trite as that sounds. You must start off by fighting for the opportunities to help with or position yourself for trial roles. You must learn to be a trial attorney too by going to courses, going to programs, going to the trial academy, taking drama classes, going to trials to watch them, reading transcripts of the best attorneys, all of which I did voraciously.

The attorneys who claim to want to be trial attorneys but wait complacently to get there do not strike me as the ones likely to make it to the big leagues of trial attorneys. This takes incredibly hard work but also work on your own to better yourself and to be ready to perform. You must be proactive and push yourself to do these things. You may have to wait for your day in court, but there is so much you can and should be doing in the meantime to position yourself for trial greatness when that day finally comes. I dug up trial transcripts of my mentors and of the greatest opposing counsel in Atlanta and studied their tactics and moves. There were not videos in those days or Court TV, which nowadays would make this so much easier. I also found out where the local trials were happening and tried to watch some of them to learn from the masters and my mentors in the early days of my career. I am always honored when that happens to me, and I see young attorneys watching me at trial or who reach out to me to ask for my advice. Don't be shy about doing so because nothing is more fun than sharing trial war stories especially to a mentee or young star who wants to rise in the trial world.

WJE: What is the best advice you ever received?

LGC: The best advice I ever received was way back from my mentor when I was just learning to be a trial attorney; he always told me to be myself and not try to channel him or someone I was not. Let yourself shine through in court, and I have always tried to do that for better or worse! He is the one who also told me early on in my cases to be thinking about closing argument when you are in discovery and or taking depositions. My style is to prepare and take every deposition as if it is a trial cross-examination and to hear my closing argument and my trial themes as early as in the beginning stages of discovery of a case. I never take a deposition that sounds like a deposition, but rather it sounds more like I am at trial, or it should, anyways.

WJE: What is the worst advice you ever received?

LGC: Thankfully, I have not received much bad advice or maybe I pushed it out of my mind. I guess there are those who tried to tell me that I should get away from doing medical cases early on, suggesting I would do better or go further by doing all corporate entity representations. I never thought that was true. Medical malpractice and later medical device and pharmaceutical trials are complex and involve very sympathetic plaintiffs; and I have always found them interesting and rewarding for many reasons. I stuck with medical malpractice work primarily for my first decade of practice, and I am quite grateful that I did so because I learned so much and honed my trial skills. In later years, the breadth of my trial practice broadened to include white collar, commercial litigation, consumer fraud, class action, labor and employment, environmental and toxic tort on top of my mainstay areas of products liability, medical device, and pharmaceutical. As one of my clients said when inviting me to do several serious trials of the white collar/fraud and labor/employment types, I want you and need your ability to tell a resounding story to the jury—you can learn the specialty, I am not worried about that. I have agreed with that sentiment and given how much I love a good trial and being in the courtroom and any courtroom, I am willing and enthusiastic about trying any cases that are important to any of my clients or future clients—"send me in coach," I like to say, and I meant it.

WJE: What was the most rewarding case you have handled and why?

LGC: One of the most rewarding cases I have tried is the one I described earlier from Seattle for my client Medtronic or one I tried for Medtronic even earlier, in state court in Connecticut in 2007–2008. That case was a very challenging case in a challenging venue against reportedly the toughest opposing firm in the state. The plaintiff was a young woman, 13 at the time of injury, who ended up in a persistent vegetative state or as the plaintiffs argued, a locked-in state. It was an incredibly long trial lasting over three months, and we were very pleased to attain a full defense verdict against all odds. I was in my early 40s, trying a very serious case against much more experienced adversaries on their home turf for a very important client. I learned a great deal from that trial and count that as one of the most rewarding trial experiences. Also, with the plaintiffs brought into the court in front of the jury, my empathy and ability to show it to the jury mattered. Also, I learned then the importance of "out-localing" the local attorneys by being especially respectful to all the judges and their staff in our court and around the courthouse and earning their respect by always being early, super-prepared, and knowing local rules as well as the law and facts better than anyone else.

WJE: What case caused you the most sleepless nights?

LGC: I would say the trial that was ultimately lost and overturned on appeal for a very obviously bad ruling. That ruling which impacted the trial and evidence greatly hung over our heads and haunted my dreams during that trial. I spent many sleepless nights trying to figure out what to do to both combat that ruling and still win, and to perfect our record on appeal.

The judge, contrary to the law and quite prejudicially to my client and our trial defense, excluded all evidence that our client's medical device was cleared by the FDA and thus left the jury to think that it was illegal or experimental or something was not right about it. This had significant impact on what our witnesses could say and what evidence we could show the jury as well as what I could argue.

WJE: In cases you lost, what did your opposing counsel do that you thought was effective?

LGC: In that same case, I thought the opposing counsel took full advantage of that ruling to make our company look incredibly bad and conjure up enough vilification to inspire the jury to render a plaintiff's verdict and even a punitive damages verdict. In the few cases I have lost, the opposing attorneys found ways to show my client to be a bad company, even when not true, and to use evidence, documents, and testimony out of context.

WJE: How can a young lawyer get more trial opportunities in federal court?

LGC: Young attorneys can find the attorneys trying cases like I did and make themselves available or make it known they are willing to help. At the same time, looking for ways within and outside of the firm to learn more about trials, read transcripts, watch trials, learn from the greats out there.

WJE: Do younger lawyers ask you for trial advice?

LGC: Yes, all the time. And I am always extremely honored and excited to share what I know, what I did, my journey, and of course the trial stories that always seem to grow in time but are an absolutely joy to share with anyone who asks and anyone who will listen!

7
Chaka M. Patterson
Partner, Alston & Bird, San Francisco

For almost three decades, Chaka Patterson has litigated high-stakes matters in private practice, corporate settings, and government, giving him a unique 360-degree view of how the law works. He began his legal career as a law clerk to the Honorable Solomon Oliver Jr. in the United States District Court for the Northern District of Ohio and the Honorable Karen Nelson Moore in the United States Court of Appeals for the Sixth Circuit. After falling in love with the courtroom during his clerkships, Chaka became a trial lawyer at top law firms, including Bartlit Beck, Skadden Arps, Jones Day, and Jenner & Block. Now a partner at Alston & Bird, he represents clients in business and commercial litigation and white-collar criminal defense involving state attorneys general investigations, False Claims Act (FCA) actions, and internal investigations and compliance reviews.

Prior to joining Alston & Bird's San Francisco office, he served as Senior Vice President, General Counsel, and Corporate Secretary at Adtalem Global Education. As General Counsel, he made national headlines by choosing a team of five Black women lawyers to lead Adtalem's $1.48 billion acquisition of Laureate Education, a newsworthy decision given that Black women are underrepresented in the profession: they make up only about 3 percent of the partners at law firms. Chaka also took a complete break from the courtroom by serving as Vice President, Treasury & Investor Relations at Exelon, a Fortune 100 company, where he managed the company's balance sheet, cash, bond offerings, and relationships with external stakeholders.

Chaka has significant government experience. As Chief of the Civil Actions Bureau for Cook County's State's Attorney in Illinois, he managed a team of 100 lawyers defending the county and its officeholders and employees in civil suits, serving as first-chair on several federal cases. Chaka also served as an Assistant Attorney General and Chief of the Illinois Attorney General's Office Special Litigation Bureau, where he prosecuted civil and criminal fraud cases, including health care fraud, securities fraud, complex consumer fraud, charitable trust fraud, and False Claims Act cases.

I attended Amherst College with Chaka, succeeding him as Student Body President there. Later we were classmates at Harvard Law School. Chaka thereafter earned an MBA in finance and economics from the University of Chicago Booth School of Business. He is married to Tracey Patterson, a Managing Director at Accenture, and has two daughters. I interviewed him on December 20, 2022.

Willie J. Epps Jr. (WJE): Did you always want to be a trial lawyer?

Chaka M. Patterson (CMP): Yes. My mother is a retired history professor at Northwestern University. She introduced me to books that highlighted the key participants in the civil rights movement, including the lawyers. I also saw myself in the courtroom advocating for the righteous. Then in high school I was invited to join the Constitutional Law Society and got a chance to meet "cause" lawyers, who additionally inspired me to want to become a courtroom lawyer. At Amherst College, my desire to become a courtroom advocate was stoked by the book *Black Men of Amherst*. The book profiled many of the most successful lawyers in America, who happened to be Black graduates of Amherst College, such as William H. Lewis, the first Black person to hold a senior role at the U.S. Department of Justice; Charles Hamilton Houston, who was the Dean of the Howard Law School, Thurgood Marshall's mentor, and the architect of the strategy to overturn *Plessy v. Ferguson*; and William Hastie, who was the first Black federal judge. Not only had they all attended Amherst College, but they also attended Harvard Law School.

Once I read *Black Men of Amherst*, I set my sights on accumulating as much exposure to courtroom lawyers as I could. In the summer between my sophomore and junior years in college, I interned for Judge Richard Parsons, the first Black Article III judge. There I got to see courtroom lawyers every day, five days a week, for an entire summer. After court each day, Judge Parsons, an accomplished trial lawyer before joining the bench, would educate me on what made for a good or bad performance. I also got to see several cases tried that summer, and again, Judge Parsons would help me understand what great lawyering looked like.

I got exposure to great lawyers and great lawyering during the summer between my junior and senior years in college when I interned on Wall Street in the litigation department at the law firm of Fried Frank. The Fried Frank litigators allowed me to shadow them all summer, especially when they went to court. It was an exhilarating experience to watch them perform in court and then debrief afterward.

The combination of interning for Judge Parsons and Fried Frank solidified for me that I was going to be a trial lawyer. After Amherst, like my fellow alumni legal heroes, I attended

Harvard Law School. At Harvard, I continued to accumulate courtroom experience by participating in the Ames Moot Court competition and second chairing a trial as a member of the Harvard Defenders Program.

Immediately following my graduation from Harvard, I had the honor and privilege of clerking for Judge Solomon Oliver Jr. on the federal court for the Northern District of Ohio in Cleveland. Judge Oliver was an accomplished trial lawyer, having served as a long-time Assistant United States Attorney (AUSA) in Cleveland before taking to the bench. He allowed me to sit in on all of the trials, and like Judge Parsons before him, he taught me what great lawyering looked like.

After my clerkship with Judge Oliver, I joined Jenner & Block's Chicago office as a junior associate. Jenner was then and still is considered one of the premier law firms for people who want to be trial lawyers. After all of those years of reading, watching, practicing, and preparing, I had now finally reached a place where I could become a real-life trial lawyer.

WJE: So your mother was a college professor and your stepfather is an attorney. Did either encourage you to become an attorney?

CMP: No. Remarkably, my parents wanted me to be a doctor. To this day, I still do not understand why they thought that was an appropriate career path for me. I had little interest in and even less aptitude for the hard sciences. Where I excelled was in researching, writing, and public speaking. I did not know it then, but those are some of the most essential tools for a trial lawyer. In retrospect, I now know that the hard sciences and math are great preparation for trial work. They teach you how to think logically and present complicated facts cogently. You start with a hypothesis (or thesis). You test it until you find what works and what doesn't. Then you must build a case through a set of observations (facts) to defend your hypothesis. Gee, that sounds a lot like trial work! I just didn't know it at the time.

Perhaps my subconscious knew it at the time because, to humor my parents, I took math and science all four years of high school, and I even interned for my uncle, also an Amherst alumnus, who is a pediatric cardiac surgeon. Be careful what you wish for. Any hope of my becoming a doctor quickly dissipated once I saw my uncle open up a heart—of a kid no less. Definitively set me on the trial lawyer path.

As they say, whoever "they are," hindsight is 20/20, and in hindsight, I am thrilled with my choice of becoming a trial lawyer rather than a doctor.

WJE: How did you first access the courtroom to gain experience?

CMP: Immediately following my clerkship for Judge Oliver, I joined Jenner & Block's Chicago office as an associate. Jenner had a policy that first-year associate time was not billed to clients. As a result, first-year associates could take on pro bono matters if they wanted to do so. I wanted to do so. I took on a felony criminal case in state court; a civil rights case in federal court; and a felony criminal case in the Seventh Circuit. The criminal case in state court involved Ruben Vega. Ruben was an 18-year-old Latino male.

The state had charged Ruben with felony assault and battery in connection with a fight at a party. No big deal, except for one thing—Ruben had two prior felony convictions. Under Illinois law, at the time, if convicted of a third felony, Ruben would be a Class X felon and eligible for up to a 30-year prison sentence. In other words, if I lost this case, Ruben would spend almost twice as much time in prison as he had been alive. How's that for your first case essentially fresh out of law school?!

That this was my first case fresh out of law school is exactly what I shared with Ruben in our very first meeting. I vividly remember meeting with Ruben in the conference room reserved for attorney–client meetings in the prison. I told Ruben this was my first case as a brand-new lawyer. That's the bad news . . . for him. The good news was that I was a graduate of the Harvard Law School, an associate at Jenner & Block, and I would work my ass off for him. The only thing he heard in that string of comforting words was Harvard Law School. Apparently, that's all he needed to hear, as he signed the engagement letter on the spot, and I now had my first official client.

Not having a clue about Illinois criminal law (despite having passed the Illinois bar on my first try) or anybody's law of evidence, I had to rely on my common sense. My common sense told me that I had way more time and resources than did the prosecution. So, the only strategic call I made was the one that mattered most. I insisted on my client's constitutional right to a speedy trial. Sure enough, the prosecution could never get its act together to take the case to trial. I refused to agree to any continuances, and the judge refused to grant any. As a result, the prosecution offered a plea to a misdemeanor and no jail time, which Ruben gratefully accepted.

While the Vega case did not result in a trial, it did teach me several valuable lessons. First, start with the end in mind. How do you want this case to end, and what strategic decisions can you drive to bring about that result? Second, always, always, always be prepared. When you know where you want to go and you are always prepared to go there, it is remarkable how your opponent's errors or lack of preparation can provide a window of opportunity to accelerate to your and your client's desired outcome. Third, treat everyone like they are the most important person in the world. I went out of my way to be super respectful of everyone I encountered: the jail staff, the courtroom staff, the prosecution . . . everyone. The goodwill I built up inured to my and my client's benefit and helped me reach a successful outcome.

Those lessons helped me reach a successful outcome in the civil case against the U.S. Attorney's Office for the Northern District of Illinois. I represented Romona Johnson. Ms. Johnson was in her mid-fifties and dying of cancer. The USAO was suing her for Medicaid fraud.

Like George Washington in the musical *Hamilton*, once again, I was "out gunned, out manned, outnumbered, outplanned. . . ." I definitely needed a right-hand man. Enter Josh Berman, who has gone on to a distinguished career in the law (AUSA Southern District of New York [SDNY], DOJ Public Integrity Division; he led the investigation into the FBI crime lab and is now a partner at Clifford Chance). Josh and I worked that case like it was the only thing we had to do . . . because it was! We gathered all of the documentation and witness statements to prove our client's innocence. We then insisted on and got a meeting with the USAO's Chief of the Civil Division. We presented our evidence in a respectful and compelling way and reminded her that while she had the full force of the United States government behind her, we had Jenner's virtually unlimited resources, the moral authority in that we were representing an innocent woman who was dying of cancer, and this case was literally the only case we were working on. To make our desired outcome easy on her, we brought along a motion to dismiss with prejudice for her to review. She reviewed the evidence and the motion, and filed the motion the very next day.

The Johnson case reinforced for me the importance of being thoroughly, thoroughly, thoroughly prepared, prepared, prepared. It also taught me that compelling presentations are not just for the jury, but for any decision maker. Lastly, it taught me how to be hard on the facts and law without being hard on the people. In fact, as fate would have it, a decade later, the Chief of Civil and I would be on the same side of some blockbuster cases—she was still Chief of Civil in the USAO, and I was Chief of Special Litigation in the Illinois Attorney General's Office. That collaboration would not have been possible had I presented my case to her in a contentious fashion.

Collaborating without being contentious is a lesson that was reinforced for me when I represented Ruby Lamb in the Seventh Circuit. Ms. Lamb had been convicted of a serious drug offense and using a firearm in furtherance thereof, which mandated an additional five years be added to her already lengthy sentence. Picking up the case on appeal meant I had to work with the person who had tried her case. Appellate work is essential to be a good trial lawyer because part of being a good trial lawyer is knowing how to preserve issues for appeal. A lesson Ms. Lamb's trial counsel had not yet learned. As a result, there was not a whole lot I could do for Ruby, and so her conviction and sentence were affirmed. However, shortly thereafter, the United States Supreme Court issued a decision that I believe impacted her sentence (though not her conviction). I filed a petition for rehearing and rehearing en banc. The Seventh Circuit granted the petition for rehearing and reversed her sentence on the gun charge, knocking five years off her sentence.

This experience in the Seventh Circuit taught me the importance of preserving the record on the facts and the law as trial counsel. Record preservation is as important for post-trial motions in the trial court, like a motion for a new trial or a new sentence, as it is for appeal.

Vega, Johnson, and Lamb were my first introduction to the courtroom as a practicing attorney. Those cases taught me lessons that would stay with me as I developed into a trial lawyer.

WJE: What are three things you did to become a top trial lawyer?

CMP: Worked hard, worked hard, and worked hard. There are no shortcuts, no alternative paths, no hack for becoming a top trial lawyer. Corners must be squared. First and foremost, I read daily. I read books on trying cases. I read the Federal Rules of Civil Procedure, of Appellate Procedure, and of Evidence. I read books on grammar, vocabulary, and legal writing. I read biographies of the great trial lawyers like Clarence Darrow, Thurgood Marshall (yes Marshall was every bit as great in a trial court as he was in the Supreme Court), Edward Bennett Williams, David Boies, Johnnie Cochran, and Arthur Liman. Second, I joined bar associations where I could take trial advocacy classes.

I took every trial advocacy class I could take at the Chicago Bar Association, the Cook County Bar Association, and the American Bar Association. I attended demonstrations from the experts at the various bar associations. Third, I organized my peers to come into the office on Saturdays and perform mock trials in the firm's courtroom. We used anything we could find. Old NITA cases, depositions from real cases, really anything we could get our hands on. Lastly, I chased trials. I called practitioners who had trials like my stepfather and lawyers I met through the bar associations, and asked if I could co-counsel on their trials pro bono. It was a lot trying to keep up with my paying firm caseload where I was expected to bill 2000 hours per year and then take on pro bono trials. But, as a wise man once told me, "a strong enough WHY can bear any HOW."

WJE: Everyone knows you today . . . but how were you treated decades ago when you were beginning your career?

CMP: Judges were always very respectful because my clerkships taught me how to prepare for court and how to handle myself in court. Opposing counsel was largely dismissive due to my youthfulness and race, which never bothered me because they underestimated me at their peril. As I told opposing counsel, "you will never be able to outwork me." And I have found that the person who puts in the most work is well positioned to prevail. I also found that juries appreciated my style in court. For example, I would help my "old timer" opponents with the courtroom technology of the day, and I would help them with their exhibits. Juries respected the fact that I respected my elders and acted appropriate for my age in the courtroom. I never tried to adopt a persona that was inconsistent with my age. I did not try bombast. I did not try petulance. I did not try to be obsequious. I was and still am authentic to who I am and how I like to treat people and to be treated.

WJE: What are three things a lawyer can do to win a federal jury trial?

CMP: In real estate, they say the three key things are location, location, location. Well, in winning a federal jury trial, the three key things to do are to prepare, prepare, prepare. There is simply no substitute for preparation and preparation always positions you to win. You may not always win, but you are certainly well positioned to do so through preparation. Preparation includes knowing the law, the facts, the evidence, the demonstratives, the witnesses, the jury, opposing counsel, and the judge better than anyone else in that courtroom. Preparation means everyone looks to you when they are stuck or when a difficult issue arises because they know that you will know the answer because you are always prepared for everything. Preparing for everything means thinking three moves ahead like a chess player. Having redundancies for all witness testimony, documents you want to introduce into evidence, motions you want to make. You own the courtroom like you own your home because you know where everything is and how everything works. You know who is coming and going and why.

WJE: How do you prepare and use a trial notebook?

CMP: In federal jury trials, I usually turn the final pretrial order into my trial notebook:

- Witnesses
- Exhibits and evidentiary foundations
- Jury Instructions

- Motions in Limine and other key rulings from the court
- Key motions I have made and still awaiting ruling from the court and/or ones I may want to make throughout the course of the trial

WJE: How do you prepare and use a timeline?

CMP: I think a timeline is an essential and invaluable tool. As a result, I start the timeline at the beginning of the case and supplement it as we go along. It allows me and others to follow the story of the case. As such, I use it to prepare witnesses and to prepare the case. I then decide whether the timeline is an important demonstrative at trial, and if so, whether it is helpful in the opening statement and/or closing argument. Timelines can be critical in opening statement to orient the jury to the story and can be devastating in closing argument to drive home your story to the jury.

In a civil case, I used the timeline in closing to show how the plaintiff's memory got better with time. Well . . . memories do not normally get better with time. Lies do. But memories do not. The jury ruled in my client's favor. Similarly, in a criminal case, as a prosecutor, I used a timeline to show how every time the defendant's financial advisor received a deposit from a client, the same day or the very next day, he would make a major personal purchase in the same amount as the deposit received from his clients. The jury convicted the defendant. In a criminal case I tried as a defense lawyer, I used a timeline in opening statements in support of my client's claim of self-defense by juxtaposing my client's activities on the night of the shooting with what the person he shot was doing. The jury acquitted my client.

WJE: When do you first analyze the jury instructions for a case headed to trial?

CMP: I think the jury instructions are essential to understanding what you and the other side will need to prove at trial. I like starting with this end in mind. So, I look at the jury instructions as soon as the case is filed. I use the jury instructions to prepare and supplement my proof chart. I keep the jury instructions front and center throughout discovery and preparation for trial so that we always keep in mind what we need to do to win at trial and how to prevent the other side from proving their case.

WJE: How early do you develop your case theory and case theme?

CMP: Like the great scientist I never was, I try out various theories at the beginning of the case and then continue to update, revise, and discard as my observations—the facts—dictate. As Thomas Edison famously quipped after failing 10,000 times to get the lightbulb to work, "I have not failed 10,000 times; rather I have found 10,000 ways that will not work!" Like Edison, I keep at it, until I find a way or ways that work.

With respect to the theme, I usually wait until the final pretrial order is filed and locked before developing the theme. I like to develop a theme then because I can match the theme to what the likely evidentiary proof will be.

Some of my most memorable themes:

- In a reverse conviction civil rights case I defended where the plaintiff's memory got better with time: "Memory does not get better with time."
- In a criminal case where I prosecuted a financial advisor for stealing from his clients,

I played a clip of Gordon Gekko's infamous speech from the movie *Wall Street* where he explained why greed is good. I then told the jury that the defendant acted like "Greed is good by stealing from his clients and buying personal luxury items."

- In a civil rights employment reverse discrimination case I defended where the promotion panel was composed of all women and a male employee sued, I told the jury that "the office picked the best of the best to pick the best of the best."
- In a prisoner civil rights case I defended where the prisoner sued the prison for failing to comply with the Americans with Disabilities Act; the prisoner complained about everything in the prison, EVERYTHING, in writing, except his ADA accommodations. Not a single complaint. I told the jury: "if the prison really was not ADA compliant where are the complaints?"
- In a civil rights case where I represented the plaintiff who had been framed by a crooked cop, I told the jury, "hurt people, hurt people."

WJE: How do you prepare your opening statement and closing argument, and when?

CMP: I like to prepare backwards. I prepare my closing argument first. Then I work backwards to what needs to happen at trial to allow me to give that closing argument. What witnesses will testify to what I want to say in closing? What documents will prove what I want to say in closing? What other evidence will be admitted for me to say that in closing? After I answer all of those questions, I prepare the opening statement.

Importantly, in opening statement, I like to be very conservative in that I only talk about what I know will come in at trial. Overpromising in opening and underdelivering at trial is one of the greatest trial sins a trial lawyer can commit. Here's why: when my opponents do that, as part of my closing, I put up a chart that shows the jury what they promised and compare it to what they actually demonstrated at trial. That is a devastating demonstrative that kills them with the jury every time.

WJE: How do you approach direct examination and cross examination?

CMP: I put my approach in two buckets. First bucket: Why is it worthwhile examining this witness? I look for one of four answers: (1) proving the elements of my case—my theory; (2) supporting my theme; (3) undermining my opponent's theory and theme; and/or (4) bolstering or undermining a witness's credibility. If one of these four elements is not present, then there is no reason to call this witness or to cross-examine this witness. Too many trial lawyers feel the need to call a witness simply because the witness is on the witness list or cross a witness simply because the witness is on the stand. DO NOT BE THAT TRIAL LAWYER.

Think about the power and credibility you gain in the following situation: Your opponent has just finished what they think is a powerful examination and then with a smirk, turns to you and says, "your witness." You pop right out of your seat, look the jury in the eye, and confidently, in a loud and slow voice, say, "I. have. no. questions. for. this. witness." Then as you slowly lower yourself back into your seat, you turn your head toward your opponent in a way that only they can see you and wink. No, sorry not sorry. Don't ever wink at your opponent or anyone else in the courtroom. But you get my point. Examine witnesses only when the examination moves you toward victory or your opponent toward defeat.

Second bucket: Don't be a regular lightbulb either all the way up or all the way off. Instead, be a lightbulb with a dimmer switch where the light can be adjusted for your needs and the mood you want to set. Many trial lawyers, like the regular lightbulb, only have one courtroom style regardless of what's happening around them or who they are examining. DON'T BE THAT TRIAL LAWYER. Be the trial lawyer who is like the lightbulb on the dimmer switch. Adjust your brightness depending on the mood you are trying to set and the needs of your case. You have to have a different approach to examining a child witness than you would an adult. You have to have a different approach to examining a rape victim than a hardened criminal who has been promised a deal in exchange for their testimony against your client. A jury full of engineers, mathematicians, and bankers is unlikely to be persuaded by theatrics and bombast as much as by hard evidence and logical reasoning. Accordingly, great trial lawyers vary their approaches to examination, depending on the witness and depending on the jury. BE THAT TRIAL LAWYER!

WJE: How many cases have you tried to verdict? How many in federal court? Civil and criminal?

CMP: I have tried 15 jury trials to verdict and 5 bench trials to verdict. Most of my trials have been civil and in federal court. Most of my state court trials have been criminal, either prosecution or defense. I enjoy jury trials in federal court the most. I enjoy jury trials because it always amazes me that we literally get to pick our decision makers. I love the jury selection process. Getting to interact with these strangers, finding a way to make these strangers comfortable with you, with each other, and with the courtroom, getting them to open up to you in front of a courtroom full of other strangers in a way that feels good, and establishing yourself as the "go to" person, the person that knows what they are doing right from the outset. It is an exhilarating feeling.

I like federal court because there are rules and procedures that are tried and true and vary little from courtroom to courtroom. The federal rules and the federal judges try to be the best of what our adversary system is—everyone working from the same set of rules and procedures and same set of facts—the advocates can focus on advocating when trial by ambush is eliminated.

WJE: Let's talk about your high-profile cases. Describe what you did to win. Please give details of any interesting trial moments.

CMP: 1. I sued the State of Illinois on behalf of a prisoner, who had an epileptic seizure and fell out of the top bunk bed and sustained serious injuries. The prison knew he was an epileptic and knew he was supposed to be in a low bunk close to the floor. The guards exhibited deliberate indifference to his serious medical need. We did two things to win: (1) We won two significant pretrial rulings: (i) we were able to exclude why our client was incarcerated; and (ii) because we were handling the case pro bono, the State had to pay for us to get an expert. (2) The order of witnesses. We called our expert on epileptic seizures and were able to introduce a video through the expert on what a person experiencing a seizure looked like. It was powerful testimony and evidence. We then called the defendant correctional officers (COs) in our case-in-chief as adverse witnesses. We knew they would be in the courtroom to see the video because they would be parties seated at the defense table. We knew the jury would be looking to see if the COs displayed any emotion and would be anxious to hear from the guards immediately. It worked. We went after the guards hard, and each of the guards just came across as if they literally did not care. One after the other. In fact, I got the supervisor to say on the witness stand that she did not care about any of the prisoners under her care—that was a Perry Mason moment—especially after seeing the video. We then called our client and slow-walked him through the terror of climbing into that top bunk every night knowing that when (not if) he had a seizure, he would fall out of that bunk and seriously hurt himself for no reason other than the fact that the guards would not put him in the lower bunk. It was powerful testimony. It was a weeklong trial and the jury came back in two hours. It was the first prisoner civil rights victory in the state of Illinois. The state settled on appeal for the full amount of the damages verdict because they did not want an unfavorable 7th Circuit opinion on the books.

2. I defended the State of Illinois's affirmative action in a contracting program against a constitutional challenge. I called the beneficiaries of the program to tell their stories and how they had been shut out of contracting before the advent of the program and

what a difference the program had made in their businesses, in their lives, and in their communities. I also called White contractors who testified to the excellent work done by the beneficiaries of the program. We told a very effective story at trial. Then in closing, I used technology where I put the wording of the statute on the screen, and then redlined it the way the plaintiff wanted it to read and explained to the court that courts do not redline statutes, that courts apply statutes as written. As written and as applied, the statute was constitutional. The trial court ruled in our favor and the 7th Circuit affirmed.

3. I defended the Cook County Public Defender's Office and three female supervisors against a reverse discrimination case brought by a male public defender, who alleged he was not promoted solely because he was a male and the selection panel was comprised of the three female defendants. We did three things well: (1) I crossed the plaintiff by using courtroom technology to project his application side-by-side with the applications of the male public defenders who were promoted—His application did not measure up at all. A typical question and answer session went like this:

   Mr. Plaintiff do you see your application on the left?
   Yes.
   Do you see Mr. X's application on the right?
   Yes.
   Do you know Mr. X?
   Yes.
   Mr. X is male, correct?
   Yes.

Mr. X was assigned to the same courtroom as you, correct?
Yes.
Mr. X has tried 25 jury trials, correct?
Yes.
You have tried 5 jury trials, correct?
Yes.
Mr. X has written 7 articles, correct?
Correct.
You have not published any articles, correct?
Correct.
Mr. X has given 10 speeches, correct?
That's what it says.
You have given no speeches, correct?
Correct.
Mr. X was promoted, correct?
Yes.

Also, whenever the plaintiff tried to wiggle out of answers, I impeached him by playing the relevant part of his deposition. It is simply devastating to be impeached with a video deposition. The witness just looks dumb denying something and then watching themselves say that exact thing on videotape. I did that twice, and the plaintiff never fought me again. (2) I called each of the three female defendants and took them through their long and storied careers as public defenders, why they were selected to serve on the promotion panel, and how they made the selections; and (3) In closing, I hit my theme by standing behind each of my clients and going through her credentials (30 years as a public defender, 50 homicide jury trials, supervisor in the office, awards received from all of the local bar associations), and then I walked over to the jury box and said, "the best of the best, picked the best of the best." I then explained that there was nothing wrong with the plaintiff, he simply was not the best of the best to go to the next level similar to how there are many great collegiate athletes who despite their success in college are not good enough to get to pros. The jury ruled in our favor—complete defense verdict. The judge as we were packing up told me that was one of the best closing arguments he had seen because the themes clearly resonated with the jury.

4. I defended the head of the criminal division of the Cook County State's Attorney's Office who was sued in a wrongful conviction case brought by a person who had been in prison for 21 years for a crime he did not commit. The plaintiff also sued the police officers who interrogated him. My strategy at the outset was to sit back and let the plaintiff take big swings at the police officers. I literally wanted the jury to forget that we were even in the courtroom, consistent with my theory of the case that we should never have been in the case because we had no interaction with the plaintiff. The only thing we did in the seven- week trial was cross the plaintiff. That cross yielded all I needed for my closing theme—the plaintiff's story kept getting better and better with time and more detailed, and then he eventually added my client as a defendant. So, my theme in closing was "memory does not get better with time . . . lies do . . . but memory does not." I put up a timeline of everything the plaintiff had ever said about his wrongful incarceration and showed how his memory kept getting better

with time. The jury found against the police for $13M. The jury found my client not liable. The jury verdict was affirmed on appeal.

5. In a criminal case I tried as a prosecutor, we prosecuted a financial advisor for fraud. Inexplicably, he decided to testify in his own defense. On cross, I used technology to put up each and every fraudulent transaction, and then I proceeded to break the cardinal rule of cross by asking open-ended questions. I asked the defendant to read the transaction, and then I asked him to tell the jury who he purchased the item for. For example. Defendant read transaction #1 to the jury: purchased a Range Rover for Jane Smith. Tell the jury who Jane Smith is. My mother. Then I switched back to a cross question: The victim did not authorize you to spend her money on a Range Rover for your mother, correct? Remarkably, he responded "correct." It was hilarious. I also used a timeline to show that he made personal purchases immediately following a deposit by a client with his firm. The jury was out for like an hour before convicting the guy.

WJE: Please explain the different types of trial lawyers you have observed through the years. Which kinds are most effective in front of a jury?

CMP:

1. The Theatrical lawyer who thinks they are Perry Mason or Clarence Darrow.
2. The Technical lawyer who puts in their evidence without any flare or flavor.
3. The Blustery lawyer who fights like hell over everything and tries to be the super tough person.
4. The Smooth talker who thinks they can charm jury into a verdict.

5. The Authentic lawyer who presents in front a jury like they are in their living room talking to an old friend.

I think the Authentic lawyer presents the best in front of a jury. Jurors are very smart and very perceptive. They know when someone is putting on a persona versus when a person is being genuine. They see how the trial lawyer treats the court, the court staff, their own staff, opposing counsel, people in the pews, etc. How you treat those around you says a lot about who you really are, and jurors pick up on that.

WJE: How do you deal with bad advice from co-counsel?

CMP: I have found that there must be a first chair. You cannot really have co-counsel for this very reason. Someone has to be empowered to make the final call and live with the consequences of making that call.

WJE: What is the best way to develop into a top trial attorney?

CMP: Try as many cases as possible. Learn from your wins and your losses. Read as much as possible about trials and trial techniques. Teach as much as possible. It's incredible how much you learn from teaching others. Stay humble.

WJE: What is the best advice you ever received?

CMP: Try as many cases as possible. Learn from every trial. Do not be afraid to lose. The trial lawyer who proclaims to have never lost a case has not tried enough cases. Trying cases is like running marathons. You cannot proclaim to be a great marathoner or even a marathoner of any renown, having only run one. You must run multiple marathons, learn from each one, and add and subtract from your repertoire as you learn and grow.

WJE: What is the worst advice you ever received?

CMP: Great trial lawyers can take any random set of 12 in the box and win. No. That is simply not true. The greatest part of our jury trial system, to me, is that you get to pick your decision maker. If done correctly, you have already won by picking the right set of decision makers. If done poorly, there is almost nothing you can do to overcome jurors who are against you.

I learned this lesson the hard way. I represented a plaintiff who was suing a dirty cop for framing him. My client spent 400 days in jail for a crime he did not commit. We had a compelling case. Only one problem—my "co-counsel," who was first chair, ignored my advice and allowed a nurse to stay on the jury instead of exercising a peremptory strike. In my view, nurses are not who you want on a jury in a tort case—civil rights, personal injury, does not matter—because they see medical professionals (their friends and colleagues) sued all of the time and are therefore generally biased against plaintiffs in tort cases. I was right. The nurse was the foreperson. The jury ruled in favor of the cop. Fortunately, this story had a happy ending. The trial judge made some bad evidentiary rulings, which we appropriately preserved for appeal. On appeal, the Seventh Circuit reversed and remanded for a new trial. On the eve of the retrial, the cop settled.

WJE: What was the most rewarding case you have handled and why?

CMP: The James Newsome case. Newsome had been in prison for 15 years for a homicide he did not commit. James was eventually pardoned after getting his case heard by the U.S. Supreme

Court, representing himself pro se. James asked me to take the case to trial after he lost confidence in the lawyers representing him. Those lawyers wanted him to take a settlement of $90,000. Everyone was sure the case was a loser because three witnesses had picked James out of a lineup. My point was that there was no chance three people picked out the same wrong guy without corrupt police interference. The case went to trial while I was an associate at Bartlit Beck. Phil Beck gave the closing and noted this very point. The chances were one in a million or something like that. Phil used a demonstrative of a poster board with a white background and black circles on it. There was one green dot on the demonstrative. One in a million was like finding the green dot on that poster board. The jury could never find that dot. The judge could not find the dot. I put the dot there and could not find it. No one could find that damn dot! As a result, the jury loved that exhibit and awarded James $15 million, which the Seventh Circuit affirmed. At the time, 2001, it was the largest jury verdict in history in a civil rights case. We were able to get justice for James and opened the door to other plaintiffs' lawyers coming into the space to handle wrongful conviction cases. Chicago is now the epicenter for that kind of work, and it all started with the Newsome case.

WJE: What case caused you the most sleepless nights?

CMP: The wrongful conviction case I described above. My client had just been promoted to Chief of the Criminal Division. If the jury ruled that he had framed the plaintiff for a crime the plaintiff did not commit, his whole career as a prosecutor would be called into question, his reputation for integrity [would be lost forever], and he likely would have been investigated by the office, the bar, and others. So, I felt like I literally had this guy's career in my hands. Any false or wrong move, and I could literally cost him everything he had worked so hard for. His wife and kids might look at him differently, his neighbors, etc. It was a lot of pressure, especially since he was a very accomplished trial lawyer in his own right. Being a trial lawyer representing a trial lawyer, whose very livelihood and reputation are at stake is no small undertaking. Fortunately, we won. That was the "memory does not get better with time" case.

WJE: In cases you lost, what did your opposing counsel do that you thought was effective?

CMP: They told a compelling story. It took me a while to get the hang of telling a story through opening, closing, and through witness testimony and exhibits (especially demonstratives). In each of the cases I have lost, I either did not tell a story or I told it poorly. Juries, like any audience, like to know who to root for. Who are the good guys and bad guys in this story and why? Failing to tell a compelling story that allows the jury to root for your client is fatal.

WJE: How can a young lawyer get more trial opportunities in federal court?

CMP: I'll end the way I started. A strong enough WHY can endure any HOW. Recognizing that many young lawyers have large loans to pay off, it is still necessary to go to where the trials are: Certain trial sections of the DOJ, U.S. Attorney's Offices, or federal defenders' offices. If you really think you cannot afford to work in the public sector, then you will have to meet your billable requirement and look for opportunities to serve as CJA panel counsel, or take cases pro bono from your state AGO, county, or city as those entities get sued early and often in federal court and often have more trials than people to handle those trials.

WJE: Do younger lawyers ask you for trial advice?

CMP: Yes. I enjoy teaching trial advocacy, and many of my former students call me for advice. For those of us who care about trial work, it is incumbent upon us to invest in the next generation by teaching, lecturing, supervising, lending an ear, doing anything we can to help the next generation of trial lawyers.

8

John W. Kurtz

Partner, Hubbard & Kurtz, Kansas City

John Kurtz is a product of the very best of rural Missouri. Born in 1947 in Maryville, Nodaway County, Missouri, he was raised and educated in three distinct, unique towns: Maryville, St. Joseph, and Columbia. He graduated from Columbia's Hickman High School in 1965, earned a bachelor's degree in psychology from the University of Missouri in 1969 and a master's degree in criminology from the University of Pennsylvania in 1970, just before serving in the enlisted ranks of the United States Army in Kaiserslautern, West Germany, from 1970 to 1972. Following active-duty service, John worked for the Northwest Missouri Law Enforcement Assistance Council in Kansas City, helping to disburse federal funds for criminal justice. There he crossed paths with Russell Millin, the Chair of the Council and former U.S. Attorney for the Western District of Missouri, and Council member Paul Vardeman, a Circuit Judge of the Jackson County Circuit Court. John then entered law school at the University of Missouri on the G.I. Bill, staying in touch with Judge Vardeman as he went through law school.

In 1976, after graduation, John took and passed the Missouri bar exam but found that he wanted nothing to do with the law. So, he did social work, helping disadvantaged children and the elderly through St. Augustine's Episcopal Church in inner-city Kansas City. When the job at the church ended after two years, he was at a loss as to what to do next. He reached out to Judge Vardeman who offered him a judicial clerkship, which was followed by service as an Assistant Public Defender for Jackson County from 1979 to 1981. His clients were indigent defendants in both juvenile and adult court.

John entered private practice in 1981 at the Popham law firm in Kansas City where clients included plaintiffs and defendants in civil litigation, children and adults in family law matters, and some defendants in criminal cases. In 1998, he left Popham to create what is now Hubbard & Kurtz LLP at 1718 Walnut in Kansas City.

John has tried 84 jury cases and has argued 36 appellate cases. The Missouri Bar Foundation has awarded him the Lon O. Hocker Memorial Trial Lawyer Award and the Pro Bono Lawyer Award. In 1999, Jackson County, Missouri, lawyers elected him to serve from 2000 through 2005 as a member of the 16th Judicial Circuit Nominating Commission, a group that interviews judicial candidates and submits three nominees to the Governor of Missouri.

The *Daily Record* selected him as one of Kansas City's 10 legal leaders in 2004, the Kansas City branch of the NAACP presented him the Harold Holliday Civil Rights Award in 2010, and the Kansas City Metropolitan Bar Association honored him with the Dean of the Trial Bar Award in 2015. His community service includes the boards of directors for both Genesis School and the Community Movement for Urban Progress (MOVE-UP).

John and Patricia Kurtz were married in 1987. Patricia taught at Liberty High School and William Jewell College. She also was an elected member of the Kansas City, Missouri Board of Education. They have 20 Godchildren.

I interviewed John on December 5, 2022.

Willie J. Epps Jr. (WJE): Did you always want to be a trial lawyer?

John W. Kurtz (JWK): Absolutely not! I had zero desire along that line through college graduation with a degree in psychology (University of Missouri) and a master's degree in sociology (University of Pennsylvania).

Then, after being drafted into the Army and consequently losing my Pennsylvania scholarship and then eventually being discharged from the Army, I came to Kansas City and did some work for a grant agency where I saw some lawyers in action. Two who come to mind are F. Russell Millin who was appointed the United States Attorney for the Western District of Missouri by President John F. Kennedy and Sidney Willens who was a private lawyer in a small office practice. Both of these people were dedicated to the life challenges of others. I was inspired by them, and I am grateful to God that I had the experience to see them. Watching them in action caused me to believe that it might be a good idea for me to use the GI Bill to go to law school.

WJE: Who encouraged you to become an attorney?

JWK: No one. Not one single person ever—as best I recall. My sweet parents just were not the type to push me. They supported me so long as I was a decent and honorable son and person. My mother and father were two tremendously fantastic people for whom I had the highest regard and for whom I am eternally grateful.

WJE: How did you first access the courtroom to gain experience?

JWK: I worked for Kansas City attorney Sidney Willens, for $25 a week as I recall, in the summer of 1974—after one year of law school. The next summer, I worked for consumer crusader Ralph Nader in Washington, D.C. However, then next—after law school graduation—I got completely out of the law and did community–church social work because I was so turned off by the legal profession. When that church job that I dearly loved ended two years later, I called Judge Paul Vardeman on the Jackson County Circuit Court and asked him about the possibility of serving as a law clerk. He really did not like the idea of law school graduates serving as law clerks and had never done it. However, that sweet man [recently deceased in the autumn of 2022] was so kind as to make room for me and to allow me to be in his courtroom for the last seven months of 1978. Sitting in his courtroom, I was still skeptical about the legal profession. I particularly remember one criminal case that was tried. There was a Black defendant with a White prosecutor and Black venire members. I had read about prosecutors conniving to create all-White juries with Black defendants. I felt certain I would see that coming in that particular case. I remember Judge Vardeman announcing, "Alright, voir dire for the state." Up stood Assistant Prosecuting Attorney for Jackson County, Missouri Fred Bellemere. Here is what he said: "Your Honor, I have no questions for the panel. We will take the first 12 persons—whoever they are and I will give my six strikes to the defendant."

I was totally stunned. I had a hard time believing what I had just seen and heard. It was inspiring. Contrary to all my negativism about the law, that caused me—for the first time, as I recall—to sense that there could be—sometimes—MAGIC in the law.

WJE: What are three things you did to become a top trial lawyer?

JWK: First, I cannot agree with the characterization of "top trial lawyer." I can say three things that I did to try to be the best I could:

1. I quickly realized that I would need to work basically unlimited hours in order to keep up with the people opposing me. I did not then, nor do I now, believe that I have any

ability to even have a chance at defeating opponents unless I outwork them.

2. I tried to work on cases where I truly loved the clients and loved their case. That has not always been true, but it has become increasingly true over the years and now—at age 75—I have the blessing of it being basically 100 percent true. I LOVE all my clients.
3. I think it is probably right to say that I prayed a lot.

WJE: Everyone knows you today . . . but how were you treated decades ago when you were beginning your career?

JWK: I have no complaints about treatment. There were some times that things were not as good as I would have hoped. However, overall, I have no adverse commentary about treatment. On the contrary, I have been inspired by gracious treatment from judges and, occasionally, from other lawyers and, again occasionally, by juries.

WJE: What are three things a lawyer can do to win a federal jury trial?

JWK: (1) Exhaust herself or himself in preparation.

(2) Research the judge by asking a lot of questions around the Bar so that you can be prepared to meet that particular judge's expectations.

(3) Let the judge and jury see how much you care about your client and about the case.

WJE: How do you prepare and use a trial notebook?

JWK: I have to confess that I never had anything which I called a "trial notebook." However, I certainly had notes and documents as organized as I possibly could make them so that I could anticipate most things that would come my way at trial. Then, I kept those notes and documents readily accessible so that I would not have to be fumbling around with papers in front of the judge and jury.

WJE: You have never used a trial notebook? Your organization at trial is spectacular considering you don't use the system I swear by. I am afraid to ask but will do so anyway. How do you prepare and use a timeline, another tool that I think is essential?

JWK: Using a personal injury case as an example, I have always created a detailed chronological listing of every single thing that happened in the order that it happened and with some notes about the significance of each thing that happened.

WJE: When do you first analyze the jury instructions for a case headed to trial?

CME: The candid answer is that I probably have analyzed jury instructions in a tardy fashion too often. This very question is causing me to think my better approach going forward will be to draft the jury instructions at the same time that I draft the petition so that I am familiar with the ultimate instructions from that moment onward and so that I can build my case around them.

WJE: How early do you develop your case theory and case theme?

JWK: I would hope that I think about that during the first interview with the client, trying to picture and imagine what would cause the jury and judge to have respect, and even favor, for my client, basically the plaintiff—or, in olden days, the criminal defendant.

WJE: How do you prepare your opening statement and closing argument, and when?

JWK: Again, the very excellent question causes me to realize that I have tended to do those things later than they should be done. In a dream situation, the opening statement and closing argument would be put together—at least in first draft fashion—at the same time as jury instructions are created, that being at the time of the petition being drafted for filing.

WJE: How do you approach direct examination and cross examination?

JWK: One thing I always want to avoid is arrogance. I think many jurors come to the courthouse expecting to see arrogance among lawyers and to be resistant to it. Therefore, to whatever extent I can, I try to identify myself as one more community resident—just like the jurors and their neighbors. Then, as to direct examination of my own client, I concentrate on telling a story. My sense is that jurors will be totally bored by lawyers with drifting direct examination and likewise cross-examination. I often comment on how churchgoers will sit—often bored—by the liturgy and even scripture readings. However, if the minister says something along the lines of, "This reminds me of a story . . . ," everyone seems to listen up because they are interested in stories that have beginnings and endings and heroes and villains, etc. Therefore, what I have tried to do by direct examination and cross examination has been to involve myself in storytelling in a way that will—hopefully—catch the jury's imagination and ongoing interest.

WJE: How many cases have you tried to verdict? How many in federal court? Civil and criminal?

JWK: Any type of cases tried to verdict = 85 total: 8 in federal court and 77 in state court; 12 criminal and 73 civil.

WJE: Let's talk about your high-profile cases. Describe what you did to win. Please give details of any interesting trial moments.

JWK: In August 1998, I tried a nonjury case before [U.S. District] Judge Nanette Laughrey. The name of the case was *Helen Havrum v. United*

States of America [Case # 95-4207-CV-C-5]. The case dealt with an RN at the VA Medical Center in Columbia, Missouri, who was suspected of causing the death of Mr. Elzie Havrum—a World War II veteran, Purple Heart winner, and the husband of Helen Havrum. The VA employee was suspected of taking many patients to the edge of death and then undertaking the challenge of bringing them back, but it appeared that he was unsuccessful with Mr. Havrum. Nationally known forensic pathologist Dr. Michael Baden testified for the government. The basic government defense was that the plaintiff's primary theory of codeine overdose was not valid. On cross examination, Dr. Baden acknowledged that there were multiple ways to kill persons where the means of death could never be determined. This became a foundational point in Judge Laughrey's eventual decision in favor of Mrs. Havrum and the Eighth Circuit's affirming the verdict. The winning philosophy in the case was that the nurse probably did overdose the patient with codeine. However, the circumstantial evidence was so very strong that the trial court as well as the appellate court found that the basic murder had been committed—whether by codeine or any other means. On appeal, Judge Laughrey's decision was upheld by the Eighth Circuit. When Judge Laughery had announced her decision, the entire Havrum family—who had never been seen to cry prior thereto—broke into tears . . . presumably relieved that the justice system through Judge Laughrey had recognized what had happened to Elzie Havrum in the Columbia VA Hospital.

In the Clay County Circuit Court case of *Patricia and Ronald Swope v. Todd Johnson*

[Case No. CV1018917CC]. Johnson had been charged criminally with killing his wife who was the only child of Mr. and Mrs. Swope. She was a beautiful daughter. The criminal verdict had been not guilty, but there were many facts that supported Johnson's guilt/fault. Therefore, I represented the mother and father in a civil wrongful death lawsuit despite the criminal not guilty finding. The defendant's incredible testimony was what turned the case. The dramatic moment for which I am grateful to God and which I will never forget came when the unanimous jury verdict was returned in favor of Brandy Swope's mother and father and all 12 jurors lined up to embrace the mother and father; the defendant was blocked from exiting the courtroom because of the jurors' compassion for the parents of the dead girl.

WJE: I can understand why those two cases are etched in your memory. Without commenting on opposing counsel you faced in those cases, please explain the different types of trial lawyers you have observed through the years. Which kinds are most effective in front of a jury?

JWK: Certainly, I have seen all of the following types of trial lawyers:

- Prepared and unprepared
- Arrogant and humble
- Old and young
- Women and men
- Various ethnicities

I believe the most effective ones are the generally humble lawyers who demonstrate a devotion to (even at times a love for) their clients and a devotion to their clients' causes.

WJE: How do you deal with bad advice from co-counsel?

JWK: Patiently and with my best efforts to be persuasive in terms of convincing co-counsel of something that is contrary to what they seem to think.

WJE: What is the best way to develop into a top trial attorney?

JWK:
- Work hard.
- Be prepared to work long hours.
- If you are in a position to select clients, select ones in whom you deeply believe and in fact love as fellow human beings.
- Develop the best possible relationship with clients.

These things will tend to develop the lawyer into being top-notch.

WJE: What is the best advice you ever received?

JWK: I was told by a fellow lawyer when I first started civil practice that a principle of Machiavellian philosophy was this: "Never deal an enemy a small blow."

I took this to mean that all efforts of a trial lawyer should be toward the eventual trial victory and that there should NOT be any small insults delivered to opposing counsel during the discovery process or, for that matter, anywhere, anytime. The goal needs to stay focused upon the final decision.

By the way, Google has never yet revealed to me an actual source for that exact quote, but I do continue to believe in it strongly.

WJE: What is the worst advice you ever received?

JWK: For me, every bit of advice that ever conveyed a kick-ass philosophy was something which disserved me and my clients. Unfortunately, it took me some time to realize how ultimately unproductive that approach is—at least for me.

WJE: What was the most rewarding case you have handled and why?

JWK: I did mention above one case where I represented a mother and father who lost their only child (a daughter) through murder by the son-in-law. I represented another mother who lost her only child (again a daughter) through the fault of a lawyer who was involved in an extramarital affair with the young lady lawyer and who ultimately caused her death. To have represented two mothers who lost their only children (both children being daughters) and those two mothers therefore having to live out their lives with only memories—well, those two cases deeply touched my heart.

WJE: What case caused you the most sleepless nights?

JWK: The possibility of missing deadlines, committing malpractice, and generally—in any way—letting down my clients.

WJE: In cases you lost, what did your opposing counsel do that you thought was effective.

JWK:

- Capturing the judge's mind and thereafter some critical rulings against me.
- Somehow capturing the jury's heart, mind, and soul—despite my best efforts to get a contrary result.

WJE: How can a young lawyer get more trial opportunities in federal court?

JWK: Certainly, the criminal law has always seemed to provide more opportunities for trial than civil law. Probably, going into a giant law firm at the bottom rung is not a good way to get trial opportunities in federal court. A sole practitioner or a small office practitioner would generally have a better chance for such trial opportunities. And someone involved in criminal prosecution or criminal defense would most likely have a better chance for more extensive trial experience.

WJE: Do younger lawyers ask you for trial advice?

JWK: Sometimes but not tremendously often. That infrequency probably reflects good judgment on their part.

9
Keith A. Cutler
Partner, James W. Tippin & Associates, Kansas City

Keith Cutler stars as a judge on national television, but in real life, he is a top trial attorney and a partner in the law firm of James W. Tippin & Associates in Kansas City, Missouri, where he defends civil cases. During his almost 35 years of practice, Keith has first-chaired over 80 civil trials, and has argued before numerous courts of appeals. He was the very first African American to be awarded the prestigious Lon O. Hocker Memorial Trial Award, given annually to three lawyers across the state of Missouri under the age of 36 who have demonstrated unusual proficiency in the art of trial advocacy. He has been named one of the 30 Power Defense Attorneys in Missouri by Missouri Lawyers Weekly, has obtained top defense verdicts, and has been named one of the "Best of the Bar" by the *Kansas City Business Journal*.

Keith's wife, Dana Tippin Cutler, co-stars as a judge with him on the two-time Emmy-nominated, nationally syndicated daytime television courtroom show "Couples Court with the Cutlers," which features couples who are having conflicts, complications, or disagreements in their relationships. But in reality, Dana is his law partner at the family firm founded by Dana's father, and the two are parents of three adult sons. Keith and Dana are a Morehouse-Spelman couple who both earned JD degrees from the University of Missouri-Kansas City School of Law.

I met Keith in 1998 when we were active with the ABA Young Lawyers Division, and we have been close friends ever since. Today, Keith is a member of the ABA House of Delegates and an officer of the Kansas City Metropolitan Bar Association. I interviewed him on January 2, 2023.

Willie J. Epps Jr. (WJE): When did you realize that you wanted to be a lawyer?

Keith A. Cutler (KAC): I first really started thinking about being a lawyer in junior high school, around seventh or eighth grade. So I guess I was about 12 or 13 years old.

WJE: Who encouraged you to become an attorney?

KAC: The suggestion that I should think about becoming a lawyer actually came from two different vectors. Growing up, I usually got the best and most difficult speaking parts in school and church plays because I could memorize the parts, I didn't get nervous on stage, and the teachers thought I spoke well. So, a few teachers over the years would make comments like "you know, the way you speak in public, you'd make a good lawyer or something." The seed was also planted by some of my friends because I would find and point out the inconsistencies and illogic in things they would say, and I could successfully poke holes in almost any arguments they made. Frustrated, my friends would say things like, "Man, you think you're a lawyer," or "Why do you like to argue so much? You should be a lawyer or a judge." Once I decided that I wanted to become a lawyer when I grew up, my parents, brother, and other family members fully supported and encouraged me.

WJE: How did you first access the courtroom to gain experience?

KAC: While I was in law school, I clerked at my current firm for two years before joining as a lawyer upon graduation. During that time, I would accompany our senior partner to various hearings, so that I could learn how the courtroom process works and how hearings are conducted. As a new associate, I would second-chair our senior partner in trial, which gave me up-close, hands-on experience in trial practice.

WJE: What are three things you did to become a top trial lawyer?

KAC: One thing I did as a new lawyer to help develop my trial skills was to read trial practice treatises. Over the lunch hour, instead of going out for lunch, I would eat at my desk and read books on giving opening statements, cross examining witnesses, how to get your evidence admitted, effective closing arguments, etc. Anything I could get my hands on relating to trial practice, I would read. Another thing that helped hone my trial skills was, because I was working in a small firm, I got a chance to handle every aspect of trial preparation, from crafting opening statements and legal arguments on evidentiary issues, down to collating and stapling documents and marking trial exhibits. That process helped me to become intimately familiar with every fact, every document, every piece of evidence, every argument and counter-argument, every aspect of my cases. That may not work or be feasible for everyone, but it has worked for me. A third thing that has helped me tremendously is that I went to as many trial practice CLEs [continuing legal education seminars] as my firm could afford to send me to. I gained invaluable information and practice pointers listening to seasoned lawyers and judges give presentations on what they have experienced, what they've seen, the lessons they learned, what to do, and what not to do.

WJE: Everyone knows you today . . . but how were you treated decades ago when you were beginning your career? Did more doors open for you because of your father-in-law's reputation in the profession?

KAC: When I started out as a lawyer in the late 1980s, I had five strikes against me: I was a new lawyer; I had a very youthful appearance; I was African American; I was with a small, family-owned firm that no one had really heard of; and I was in practice areas (commercial litigation, bankruptcy) in which small, minority-owned firms in the Midwest at that time typically did not practice. So, when I would appear in court or depositions and make comments, statements, or arguments, they were often dismissed or not given much weight. It was never expressly stated, of course, but the reaction I would often get was, "Well, we've practiced in this area of law for years, and we've never heard of you or your firm; you're young and inexperienced, so you probably don't know what you're talking about, so. . . ." My father-in-law's reputation did help some, probably more with judges that I appeared in front of. He was always prepared for hearings and trials; very respectful of the court, counsel, and the court staff; and always presented himself well. So, when judges found out that I was his son-in-law, they had reason to believe that I had probably been trained well.

WJE: What are three things a lawyer can do to win a federal jury trial? How does federal court differ from state court?

KAC: Federal court differs from state court in that federal court cases move a little faster, the deadlines are tighter, and the rules are stricter. For attorneys who do not fare well in federal court, it is usually due to their unfamiliarity with the rules and deadlines, more so than the merits of their cases. So for an attorney to increase their chances of winning a federal jury trial, they need to (1) make sure they're familiar with the federal rules, the court's local rules, and each judge's individual rules, and know the differences among each; (2) stay ahead of the deadlines; once you get behind the eight-ball on discovery and deadlines, it is hard to catch up, and you head into trial preparation constantly playing catch-up instead of focusing on how to best present your case at trial; and (3) recognize that the jury pool for federal court is wider, that is, generally more suburban and rural, than a state court jury pool in that same locale. So your evidence, arguments, theme, and presentation all need to be tailored accordingly.

WJE: How do you prepare and use a trial notebook?

KAC: My trial notebook is my bible during trial. Everything I think I might need to access on a moment's notice during the trial is included, for example, witness names, exhibit list, case citations for anticipated evidentiary objections, key pleadings, pretrial rulings. I usually start assembling my trial notebook at about the time I start buckling down for more intense, focused trial preparation, which is anywhere from 30 to 60 days out, depending on the complexity of the case. Because trials are dynamic, I am adding and removing items from my trial notebook as needed even as the trial is going on.

WJE: How do you prepare and use a timeline?

KAC: I take the court's scheduling order, and from that, I prepare a chronological timeline chart showing what is due and when it is due. I keep a copy on my desk that I regularly refer to, and there is a copy in our office tickler system, which alerts me when a deadline is approaching. In a more complex case where I have either co-counsel or multiple support staff working with me, I will use a task-based deadline chart, which helps me keep track of when the task assignments I have made are due to me.

WJE: What about a timeline of events for the jury?

KAC: Do I ever use a timeline for the jury? The answer is "Yes." I find a timeline helpful in presenting information to the jury. It depends on the case and on how crucial the chronology of events happens to be. The trial I am now preparing for, has a PowerPoint calendar of events because the sequence is important.

WJE: When do you first analyze the jury instructions for a case headed to trial?

CME: If it is a type of case I have handled before, I will review the jury instructions for the first time about 60 days out from trial, just to make sure there have not been any revisions to the pattern instructions. If it is a type of case I have not handled before, I will review the jury instructions much earlier in the process, like when I am drafting the petition or the answer, depending on whether I represent the plaintiff or the defendant.

WJE: How early do you develop your case theory and case theme?

KAC: It really depends on the case. In some instances, the theme and theory of the case are self-evident; it just jumps out at you from the beginning. For other cases, a compelling theme and theory may not fully come into focus until a month before trial because key facts did not become known until discovery was completed. Obviously, the earlier in the process you can develop a theme, the better; but it doesn't always work out that way. There have been some cases where I have struggled to find a viable, compelling theme until just a few days before the start of trial. I knew what I wanted and needed to prove at trial; I just had difficulty trying to work it into a theme that I thought would resonate with a jury.

WJE: How do you prepare your opening statement and closing argument, and when?

KAC: I'm usually on the defense side, so I prepare my opening statement by figuring out what it is that I need to tell the jury so that they do not immediately side with the plaintiff. There are usually enough defense-favorable facts that I can address in opening statement to make the jury think, "Okay, now I see why we're here." Sometimes I lay out my whole case—all cards on the table, so to speak. Most times, though, my openings are just to make sure that the jury understands our theme and theory of the case, and the jury is still neutral when the opening statements are done, and the plaintiff's first witness is called. As for when I start preparing my opening statement, it is usually later in the process than it probably should be. I normally start outlining an opening statement about a week or two before trial, and continuously revise and finetune, probably up to the morning of trial.

I used to write my closing arguments before the start of trial, somewhat in conjunction with my opening statements. But I kept finding that, when it came time to present closing arguments, what I needed and wanted to say was different than what I had written because of how the evidence came in. So now, I loosely outline my closing arguments and make notes during trial about what I think I need to say in closing, based on what the witnesses say on the stand and on the evidence that is admitted. Then, the night before I think we're going to do closing arguments, I pull together everything I want to say and craft it into what I hope is a compelling and persuasive view of the evidence and the law.

WJE: How do you approach direct examination and cross examination?

KAC: My overall approach to direct examination and cross examination is to focus on getting the information I need from the witness in the clearest and most efficient manner. Of course, the method to achieve that objective will vary from witness to witness because some witnesses are easier to get information from than others; so I have to adapt my approach accordingly. It is easy to get caught up in the drama and theater of direct and cross, such that when you sit down, you realize that you put on a good show, but you didn't get all the information you needed from the witness. So I try to be very careful to make sure I get all that I need from the witness while still keeping it interesting for the jury.

WJE: How many cases have you tried to verdict?

KAC: I have tried between three and four dozen jury trials and probably an equal number of bench trials. I don't practice criminal law; all my trials have been civil cases. I have had a couple of trials in federal court, but the bulk of my trials have been in state court in Missouri and Kansas.

WJE: Let's talk about your high-profile cases. Describe what you did to win. Please give details of any interesting trial moments.

KAC: I had a case that was one of the Top 10 Defense Verdicts in Missouri that year, as reported by

Missouri Lawyers Weekly. I was defending a rear-end accident case, which are not always easy cases to defend. Liability was contested primarily because there was a phantom vehicle involved which caused everyone—both plaintiff and defendant—to immediately slam on the brakes. But damages were also contested, as we believed plaintiff was greatly exaggerating her alleged injuries. So I stuck to my guns; I refused to concede liability, and I hammered away at plaintiff's credibility by using her own medical records against her to contradict her testimony. She came across as a nice lady, so I had to be careful in how I cross-examined her. I just gently and methodically continued to point out how her testimony about the extent and continuing nature of her injuries was not supported by her medical records.

WJE: Please explain the different types of trial lawyers you have observed through the years. Which kinds are most effective in front of a jury?

KAC: The trial lawyers I have been in trial with vary greatly in style and approach. Some are very aggressive; some are laidback and even keeled; some are highly organized and efficient, while others are constantly fumbling with documents and appearing disoriented à la "Columbo" (the 1970s TV detective series starring Peter Falk). I don't know that there is one style that is more effective in front of a jury than another. I have seen aggressive trial lawyers be effective in front of one jury, but that same style alienates a jury in another trial. Broadly speaking, jurors like attorneys who know what they're doing, who come across as sincere and earnest, and who treat everyone with respect and decency. And I have seen both aggressive and laidback attorneys fit that bill. So, I tell law students and newer trial attorneys that they have to find a style that fits their own personality. They can watch and learn from other trial attorneys, but they should not try to emulate someone else or adopt a "trial persona" that doesn't fit them. The jury will see right through that, usually to the detriment of the attorney and their client.

WJE: How do you deal with bad advice from co-counsel?

KAC: Bad advice from co-counsel is tricky to deal with because it depends on your level of authority relative to your co-counsel. If I am the first chair, then I evaluate advice from my second chair co-counsel through the lenses of my own experience, my understanding of the law and facts, my assessment of my co-counsel's experience and knowledge, and my analysis of the probable outcomes of following or not following their advice. Then I make the best decision I can under the circumstances. If I am the second chair, I probably go through the same analysis but recognize that ultimately it is not my decision to make whether or not to follow the advice. I can lobby for my position and explain why I think the first chair's advice is bad, but at the end of the day, the first chair has the greater responsibility to the client and has to ultimately answer to the client for whatever decision is made.

WJE: What is the best way to develop into a top trial attorney?

KAC: The best way to develop into a top trial attorney is to learn the law; learn the rules of civil procedure; watch top trial attorneys in action—in depositions, hearings, as well as in actual trial; have mentors who can alert you to all the customs, practices, and "unwritten rules" you need to know as a trial attorney; talk to judges about the good and bad techniques they've seen lawyers use in court; and last of all, try cases. The more you do something, generally speaking, the better you become at it. That last one is the most difficult to do because when you get to try a case and how many you get to try is beyond our control as trial attorneys. It depends on an attorney's work environment, the client's willingness to go to trial, the financial viability of the case, the court dockets, and several other factors. But regarding the other things I mentioned, those are within the control of most up-and-coming trial lawyers. The bottom line to all of this is that, in order to become a top trial attorney, you have to put the work in. There are no shortcuts. It requires many hours of reading, studying, learning, observing beyond your normal workload with your firm or office.

WJE: What is the best advice you ever received?

KAC: The best advice I received as a trial lawyer is probably "try your own case." Sometimes we get so hung up and focused on what the other side is going to do that we spend a lot of time and energy responding to and trying to deflect that, instead of making sure the strong points of our own case come through. I'm not suggesting that you can completely ignore opposing counsel's evidence and arguments; you have to be aware of what they're going to do and have a plan to counter it. But don't get so caught up in what the other side is doing that you lose focus on what you need to do for your case. I think that advice—from my senior partner and father-in-law early in my career—has served me well over the years.

WJE: What is the worst advice you ever received?

KAC: I can't think of anything.

WJE: What is the most rewarding case you have handled and why?

KAC: The most rewarding case I handled was a commercial litigation lawsuit over a real estate management contract. My client was owed fees under the contract, and we filed suit to recover those fees seven years after the breach occurred. Defendant argued that Missouri's five-year statute of limitations on breach of contract actions applied, so our suit was time-barred. We maintained that Missouri's 10-year statute of limitations applicable to written promises to pay money applied, so we were well within the time limit. The trial court granted defendant's motion for summary judgment; the Court of Appeals reversed the grant of summary judgment, and the Missouri Supreme Court granted transfer and took up the case. The Supreme Court held that Missouri courts had been all over the place in terms of when they applied the 5-year statute versus the 10-year statute. The Supreme Court used our case to clarify the law once and for all. This was a very rewarding case because (1) I got to argue before the Missouri Supreme Court, (2) the Supreme Court upheld the reversal of the trial court's summary judgment, effectively determining that we were correct in our analysis and application of the law, and (3) the court used our case to set precedent for future cases. It is cited as *Hughes Development Company v. Omega Realty Company*, 951 S.W.2d 615 (Mo. banc 1997). After remand to the trial court and a two-day jury trial, the jury found in our favor.

WJE: What case caused you the most sleepless nights?

KAC: The case that caused me the most sleepless nights, figuratively if not literally, was an insurance case I was defending. A fatal shooting occurred at a banquet hall, which resulted in a $5 million wrongful death verdict against the banquet hall. The banquet hall previously had insurance coverage for incidents of this type, but when its new policy was obtained a few months before the shooting, the new policy excluded coverage for assaults and batteries. The banquet hall sued its insurance agent, claiming the agent failed to procure coverage for assaults and batteries. On behalf of the insurance agent, we maintained that assault and battery coverage is an optional coverage, which the banquet hall neither requested nor paid for. Therefore, there was no legal duty to provide it, and thus no legal liability for the lack of coverage. The case was exceedingly frustrating because, to me, the law was unmistakably clear that my insurance agent client had no duty or liability under the law. We had several appellate cases of long-standing precedent, including a couple of cases virtually on-point; but the trial court would not grant summary judgment. The case went to trial and the judge denied our motions for directed verdict, even though, again, I felt the law was clearly on our side that there was no legal duty. The jury ultimately found against us and awarded the banquet hall \$5.73 million. In my opinion, the jury wanted to give the banquet hall the \$5.73 million so that the banquet hall could then pay the judgment that the decedent's family had against the banquet hall. While I understood that sympathy aspect, I remained frustrated throughout the entire pendency of that case because I had clear case law on my side, no one was listening to me, and my client could not afford to have a \$5 million judgment against them. Ultimately, the case was reversed and remanded on appeal two years later. The parties eventually reached a settlement, thereby avoiding a retrial.

WJE: In cases you lost, what did your opposing counsel do that you thought was effective?

KAC: In cases that I have lost where I thought I should have won, I think the common thread has been that opposing counsel was able to tell a more compelling story than I was. There was one case I remember where opposing counsel's opening statement was so good, so much better than mine, I felt like I was back in law school in Trial Ad I. He had visual aids, he had graphics, he had photographs, all laid out in a PowerPoint that just blew mine away. I knew from that point (opening statements) forward that it was going to be an uphill battle, and it was; we lost. The only other time I felt like that was a similar situation, but it was closing argument. Opposing counsel's closing argument was a work of art—he had the jury rapt with attention to his every word. Fortunately for me, the facts of the case were so much in my client's favor that the jury basically had to find for my client. But pound for pound, opposing counsel blew me out of the water with his closing argument.

WJE: How can a young lawyer get more trial opportunities in federal court?

KAC: If a young lawyer is fortunate enough to get on with the U.S Attorney's Office or the Federal Public Defender's Office, that is the most expedient way to gain federal trial experience. If neither of those opportunities presents itself, becoming a part of the CJA panel is a great way for a young lawyer to get some federal court experience.

WJE: Do younger lawyers ask you for trial advice?

KAC: I have had a few younger/newer lawyers ask me for trial advice, but it is usually regarding a specific issue in a case that didn't turn out in their favor. So they'll ask me what I think about what happened because they want to prevent that particular occurrence from happening again. But I am not sure I have ever had a younger/newer lawyer ask me, "What things can I do to become a better trial lawyer?" I would encourage younger lawyers to do that—to ask seasoned, veteran trial lawyers what kinds of things they can do to become better trial lawyers. A lot of the information will be the same, but each veteran lawyer will also have their own unique perspective as well.

Part III

The Trial Notebook

Trial Notebook of Marion J. Maughmer

UNITED STATES

vs.

PARIS MARSHALL

Case No. 20-cr-0501-BCK

Jury Trial

November 14, 2022–November 18, 2022

United States District Court for the Western District of Missouri
Jefferson City, Missouri

The Honorable Brian C. Kays
United States District Judge

Daniel W. Hays and Kathleen D. Whitworth for the United States

Marion J. Maughmer and Russell K. Knox for Paris Marshall

Tab 1 Pretrial Matters

Rules of Jury Trial, Pretrial Checklist

Motions in Limine and Other Motions

Tab 2 Paris Marshall's Proposed

Marshall's Proposed Voir Dire

Marshall's Proposed Witness List

Marshall's Proposed Exhibit List

Marshall's Proposed Jury Instructions

Tab 3 Government's Proposed

Government's Proposed Voir Dirc

Government's Proposed Witness List

Government's Proposed Exhibit List

Government's Proposed Jury Instructions

Tab 4 Jury Selection

Chart/Strikes

Juror Profile

Tab 5 Opening Statement

Tab 6 Government's Case

Tab 7 Motion for Judgment of Acquittal at Close of Government's Case

Tab 8 Marshall's Case

Tab 9 Motion for Judgment of Acquittal at Close of All Evidence

Tab 10 Jury Instruction Conference

Tab 11 Closing Argument

Tab 1 Pretrial Matters

IN THE UNITED STATES DISTRICT COURT FOR THE WESTERN DISTRICT OF MISSOURI CENTRAL DIVISION

UNITED STATES OF AMERICA,	)	
	)	
Plaintiff,	)	
	)	
v.	)	No. 20-cr-0501-BCK
	)	
	)	
PARIS MARSHALL,	)	
	)	
Defendant.	)	

RULES OF JURY TRIAL

1. Court will normally convene at 9:30 a.m. and recess at or near 4:30 p.m. Counsel and the parties should be in the courtroom by 8:30 a.m. on the first day of trial and 9:00 a.m. on each subsequent day in order to take up any matters that need to be addressed before the jury is brought in at 9:30 a.m. The parties may expect morning, lunch, and afternoon breaks at appropriate times.

2. No food or drink is allowed in the courtroom, except for water in white, Styrofoam cups. The Court will provide counsel and the parties with appropriate cups.

3. Each party shall be dressed appropriately for Court.

4. During trial, only the attorneys and participants sitting at counsel table at the beginning of voir dire will be allowed to sit at counsel table at any point throughout trial.

5. Unless excused by the Court, counsel and all participants at counsel table shall: (a) stand as Court is opened, recessed, or adjourned; (b) stand when the jury enters and retires from the courtroom; (c) address all remarks, other than examination of a witness, to the Court instead of to opposing counsel; and (d) avoid disparaging personal remarks toward opposing counsel.

6. Except in unusual circumstances, counsel should stand when addressing the Court, being addressed by the Court, or examining a witness. *See* Local Rule 83.3(a).

7. The Court will conduct voir dire; in so doing, questions will be taken from those proposed by counsel. At the conclusion of the Court's questioning, counsel may be afforded an opportunity to pose follow-up or clarifying questions to the panel. The jury will be excused when questioning is finished and each side may move to strike for cause. The government's strikes will be made first, and then defendant's strikes will be made. The panel will be recalled and the jury will be seated and sworn.

8. Absent good cause shown, opening statements will be limited to thirty (30) minutes for each side.

9. No visual aid or exhibit shall be used during an opening statement, unless opposing counsel has been shown the visual aid or exhibit and has agreed to the use of the item during the opening statement.

10. The interrogation of each witness shall consist of: (1) direct examination; (2) cross-examination; (3) redirect examination; and (4) recross-examination. No further questioning will be permitted except by leave of Court in extraordinary circumstances.

11. Only one (1) counsel per party may examine a witness. *See* Local Rule 83.3(b).

12. Exhibits will rarely be circulated to jurors. If counsel wants the jury to see an exhibit during trial, it should be displayed in such fashion that all jurors may view it at the same time (i.e., by overhead projection, ELMO, computer projection, etc.).

13. Counsel shall request permission of the Court to approach a witness for a legitimate purpose. Once granted permission, counsel may approach the witness additional times without requesting permission to do so. However, witnesses shall be interrogated from a reasonable distance and shall not be badgered.

14. If a podium is provided, counsel may use it, but are not required to do so. However, counsel will not be allowed to intrude into the jury's space. Furthermore, no paper, object or hands of counsel shall be placed on the railing in front of the jury box.

15. When making an objection, counsel should say only "objection" plus the legal reason for the objection (i.e., leading, hearsay, etc.). If objecting counsel desires to give reasons for the objection or if an opposing counsel desires to oppose the objection, counsel shall request leave to approach the bench. Objections to evidence should be made only by counsel handling the witness. Objections during opening statements or closing arguments should be made only by counsel making the opening statement or closing argument.

16. After counsel questions an expert witness about his/her qualifications, do not ask the Court to declare the witness an expert.

17. Counsel shall treat adverse witnesses and parties with fairness and consideration. No abusive language or offensive personal references will be tolerated.

18. Visible reactions to a witness's testimony, counsel's presentation, or Court ruling (such as facial or body gestures) are inappropriate.

19. Do not converse with your client or co-counsel in a manner that your conversation may be heard by the jury.

20. Each party shall mark each of their exhibits prior to trial with an exhibit sticker indicating whether the exhibit is being offered by the government or defendant, along with the exhibit number. The government shall number its exhibits consecutively beginning with the number one (1). Defendant shall number his/her exhibits consecutively beginning with the number five hundred-one (501). The designation for each exhibit shall match the numeric designation for that exhibit on the exhibit list furnished to the clerk prior to trial.

21. Witnesses will remain in the witness chair unless leave of Court is granted for a witness to reference an exhibit and then the witness shall return to the witness chair immediately after referencing the exhibit. Witnesses will not be allowed to testify standing in front of the jury without leave of Court to do so. Leave will only be granted as deemed necessary and appropriate.

22. All exhibits utilized at trial as part of a party's presentation of evidence, regardless of whether admitted or not, must be kept available for use by other parties during the remainder of the trial.

23. The length of closing arguments will be established during the instruction conference.

24. The following documents shall be filed prior to the date trial is set to commence:

a. At least three (3) days prior to trial, the parties shall jointly submit an original (without sources) set and an annotated (with sources) set of proposed jury instructions to the Courtroom Deputy. Proposed annotated instructions shall reflect the authorities upon which the instruction is based and should be taken from or drawn in the manner of Model Criminal Jury Instructions for the District Courts of the Eighth Circuit and/or Missouri Approved Instructions (MAI) where available and appropriate.
b. The parties shall email the proposed jury instructions to the Courtroom Deputy. The proposed jury instructions shall be submitted in Word format. The proposed jury instructions shall be in Times New Roman, twelve (12) point font, double-spaced paragraphs, and with one-inch margins. Each proposed jury instruction shall be separated by a "page-break."

c. At least three (3) days prior to trial, counsel for each party shall file a list of proposed questions or topics counsel desires to be included in voir dire examination conducted by the Court. Objections to opposing party's voir dire questions shall be filed at least two (2) days prior to trial.

d. At least three (3) days prior to trial, counsel for each party shall agree upon a statement to be read to the jury setting forth the background of the case and the claims to be asserted. This statement will be read to the jury panel prior to voir dire. The jury statement shall be emailed to the Courtroom Deputy. The jury statement should be submitted in Word format.

25. Instructions will be read to the jury before closing arguments. Each juror will be given a copy of the instructions for use during deliberations.

26. After the jury retires, counsel for each party shall assemble all of the exhibits and keep them available in the courtroom. Counsel and their clients should remain in the courthouse and advise the Court's staff where they will be located while the jury is deliberating.

27. After the jury returns its verdict, be prepared to tell the Court if you want the jury polled.

28. After the jury is dismissed, counsel for each party must take possession of his/her exhibits from the courtroom deputy and sign the receipt at the bottom of the exhibit list.

IT IS SO ORDERED.

Date: October 10, 2022

/s/ Brian C. Kays
Brian C. Kays
United States District Judge

<u>Pretrial Checklist</u>

Are there any pending motions?

15 witnesses for the government

5–6 witnesses for Ms. Marshall

We have invoked "the rule"

Each side gets 45 minutes for voir dire following the Court's questioning.

Voir Dire for the United States: ______________

Voir Dire for Defendant: Marion J. Maughmer

We want to seat 12 jurors, 2 alternates.

We will do challenges for cause and then pick the top 22.

Each side gets 4 preemptory strikes (8 total)

That should leave us with 12 jurors, and 2 alternates.

Opening Statements: 30 minutes/30 minutes

For USA: ________________

For Defendant: Marion J. Maughmer

Any other issues:

IN THE UNITED STATES DISTRICT COURT FOR THE WESTERN DISTRICT OF MISSOURI CENTRAL DIVISION

UNITED STATES OF AMERICA,	)	
	)	
Plaintiff,	)	
	)	
v.	)	No. 20-cr-0501-BCK
	)	
	)	
PARIS MARSHALL,	)	
	)	
Defendant.	)	

MS. PARIS MARSHALL'S COMBINED MOTIONS *IN LIMINE* AND SUGGESTIONS IN SUPPORT

Ms. Paris Marshall respectfully moves the Court, *in limine*, for an Order excluding all evidence and prohibiting all questions, references, and testimony, direct or indirect, at trial and in voir dire, concerning the evidence outlined herein. In support of her Motions, Ms. Marshall states:

INTRODUCTION

On May 3, 2020, the Grand Jury returned a seven-count indictment against six individuals, including Ms. Marshall. A 17-count superseding indictment was filed on August 16, 2020. The superseding indictment charged 11 defendants in various counts with conspiracy, securities fraud, money laundering, wire fraud, and mail fraud.

Ms. Marshall voluntarily surrendered herself, and her initial appearance and arraignment were held on May 6, 2020. Ms. Marshall retained counsel. The Court released Ms. Marshall on bond on her own recognizance. On November 17, 2020, the Magistrate Judge appointed the undersigned counsel to represent Ms. Marshall. Trial will commence on Monday, November 14, 2022.

ARGUMENT

A. Motion *in Limine* to Prohibit the Government from Eliciting Testimony from any Witness that any Agreement They Signed Requires Truthful Testimony

Ms. Marshall seeks to prohibit the government from eliciting testimony from witnesses that any agreements they signed require them to be "truthful." That is to say, the government should be precluded from leading the jury to believe that the government may know something that the jury does not about the veracity of the witnesses. *United States v. Bordeaux*, 436 F.3d 900, 905 (8th Cir. 2006). Determining the credibility of witnesses is the province of the jury, and significant weight should be given to the jury's determinations. *United States v. Trotter*, 837 F.3d 864, 868 (8th Cir. 2016) ("Assessing the credibility of witnesses is a task for the jury.") (citation omitted).

During testimony, the government should be precluded from asking witnesses if they understand that their failure to provide truthful testimony may impact whether or not the government will dismiss charges, not bring charges relating to other transactions, and/or recommend a less severe sentence, which could be less than the sentencing guidelines for the crimes with which the witness is charged.

B. Motion *in Limine* to Exclude Expert and/or Agent Testimony that Invades the Province of the Jury

Ms. Marshall moves to exclude expert testimony and government agent testimony that invades the province of the jury to weigh the evidence, make credibility determinations, and fact-find. While expert testimony may be used to "assist the trier of fact to understand the evidence or to determine a fact in issue, . . . an expert witness may not usurp the jury's function to weigh evidence and make credibility determinations." *United States v. Farrell*, 563 F.3d 364, 377 (8th Cir. 2009) (citation omitted). In other words, when the jury can make a common sense evaluation of the evidence without the technical aid of an expert, such expert testimony should be excluded to prevent an expert from invading the province of the jury. *United States v. Overton*, 971 F.3d 756, 763 (8th Cir. 2020). Experts or agents should not be allowed to opine on the strength of the government's case and the credibility of its witnesses through references to the "incredible" and "strong" nature of the evidence against Ms. Marshall or any other defendant because such testimony regarding credibility or weight goes beyond the scope of proper expert testimony. *United States v. Vesey*, 338 F.3d 913, 916–17 (8th Cir. 2003).

One of the issues before the jury will be whether or not Ms. Marshall acted with specific intent in regard to the securities and wire fraud charges. Given this, the expert or agent testimony must be simply a factual conclusion rather than an attempt to express an opinion as to the knowledge, truthfulness or specific intent of Ms. Marshall. Fed. R. Evid. 704(b); *see United States v. Cowley*, 34 F.4th 636, 639–40 (8th Cir. 2022). Such impermissible expert or agent testimony would invade the province of the jury and such error would affect Ms. Marshall's substantial rights.

C. Motion *in Limine* to Prohibit the Prosecutor from Vouching for the Credibility of Witnesses

A prosecutor may not vouch for the credibility of a witness. "Improper vouching may occur when the government expresses a personal opinion about credibility, implies a guarantee of truthfulness, or implies it knows something the jury does not." *Bass v. United States*, 655 F.3d 758, 761 (8th Cir. 2011) (quoting *United States v. Roundtree*, 534 F.3d 876, 880 (8th Cir. 2008)). "[A]ttempts to bolster a witness by vouching for his credibility are normally improper. . . ." *Id.* (citation omitted). Thus, "[a] prosecutor may not place the prestige of the government behind a witness." *United States v. Mullins*, 446 F.3d 750, 760 (8th Cir. 2006) (citing *United States v. Beasley*, 102 F.3d 1440, 1449 (8th Cir. 1996)).

D. Motion *in Limine* to Preclude Sympathy or Prejudicial Argument

Counsel for the government should be prohibited from making any comment, reference, or argument, and/or putting on any evidence, designed solely to garner the sympathy of the jury or to prejudice Ms. Marshall. It is improper for counsel to indulge in an argument to the jury which tends to prejudice them towards one party or which creates undue sympathy for the alleged victims. *See, e.g., United States v. Two Elk*, 536 F.3d 890, 906 (8th Cir. 2008); *United States v. Eagle*, 515 F.3d 794, 805 (8th Cir. 2008). Government's counsel should not, for example, be permitted to ask the jury to put themselves in alleged victims' place or to make other improper arguments. Even if the Court were to sustain an objection and give a "curative" jury instruction to such remarks, Ms. Marshall would be extremely prejudiced and denied a fair trial.

E. Motion *in Limine* Regarding Size and Clients of the Law Firm Representing Defendant and CJA Appointment

Ms. Marshall is represented by the law firm of Johnson, Smith & Shook L.L.P. The Court should direct counsel for the government not to comment, either directly or indirectly, upon the size, location, reputation, or specialization of the law firm representing Ms. Marshall, or the past and/or present clients of Ms. Marshall's law firm, or other irrelevant attributes of Ms. Marshall's law firm. Also, government counsel should not be permitted to refer to defense counsel's appointment under the Criminal Justice Act. Any comment, reference, argument, or evidence of this nature should be prohibited because it is irrelevant and would serve only to prejudice the jury against Ms. Marshall and deny her right to a fair and impartial trial. *See United States v. Holmes*, 413 F.3d 770, 775 (8th Cir. 2005) ("[P]ersonal, unsubstantiated attacks on the character and ethics of opposing counsel have no place in the trial of any criminal or civil case."). Ms. Marshall requests the Court preclude the government from referring to such matters in order to avoid potentially damaging and unfair prejudice.

F. Motion *in Limine* to Exclude Statements Made during Plea Negotiations

As a general rule, statements made during plea negotiations are not admissible. Fed. R. Evid. 410; *United States v. Washburn*, 728 F.3d 775, 779 (8th Cir. 2013). The parties to this action have conducted plea negotiations. Ms. Marshall moves the Court to exclude any reference that plea negotiations occurred and to exclude any information disclosed by the parties during those plea negotiations.

G. Motion *in Limine* to Prohibit Personal Feelings of Counsel

Defendant requests the Court enter an Order prohibiting counsel from referring to their personal feelings in front of the jury regarding the case or any evidence submitted in the case. The attorneys' personal feelings are irrelevant to the factual issues in this case.

H. Motion *in Limine* to Prohibit Reference to Motions

Defendant requests the Court enter an Order prohibiting the parties from referring in the presence of the jury to any motion *in limine*, pretrial motions, other motion, oral arguments on such motions, or other matters properly kept out of the view and hearing of the jury.

I. Motion *in Limine* to Prohibit Asking Counsel to Enter into a Stipulation or for Evidence in Front of the Jury

Ms. Marshall requests the Court enter an Order precluding all parties from asking opposing counsel to enter into stipulations or requesting counsel to produce any information or documents either in their files or believed to be in their files in front of the jury.

J. Motion *in Limine* Prohibiting Reference to Declining to Enter into a Stipulation

Ms. Marshall requests the Court enter an Order precluding all parties from making any reference whatsoever to whether or not opposing counsel have declined to stipulate to any facts or have declined to agree to anything at all.

CONCLUSION

For the foregoing reasons, Ms. Marshall respectfully requests that this Court enter an Order excluding from evidence the above-referenced matters and to direct the government's counsel not to make any argument, ask any question, elicit any testimony, or otherwise make any mention, directly or indirectly, concerning any of the matters set forth above, without first approaching the bench and obtaining a ruling from the Court, outside the hearing of all prospective jurors and jurors ultimately selected, on the admissibility of such matters.

Dated: November 7, 2022

Respectfully Submitted,

JOHNSON, SMITH & SHOOK L.L.P.

By /s/ Russell K. Knox
Russell K. Knox #567892
Marion J. Maughmer #456214

10000 Highland Street
Jefferson City, Missouri 65101
Phone: (573) 980-0000
Fax: (573) 980-0001

ATTORNEYS FOR MS. MARSHALL

CERTIFICATE OF SERVICE

The undersigned hereby certifies that a copy of the foregoing was delivered on November 7, 2022, to the CM-ECF system of the United States District Court for the Western District of Missouri for electronic delivery to all counsel of record.

/s/ Russell K. Knox
Russell K. Knox #567892

Tab 2 Paris Marshall's Proposed

IN THE UNITED STATES DISTRICT COURT FOR THE WESTERN DISTRICT OF MISSOURI CENTRAL DIVISION

UNITED STATES OF AMERICA,	)	
	)	
Plaintiff,	)	
	)	
v.	)	No. 20-cr-0501-BCK
	)	
	)	
PARIS MARSHALL,	)	
	)	
Defendant.	)	

MS. PARIS MARSHALL'S PROPOSED *VOIR DIRE*

COMES NOW Ms. Paris Marshall, by and through her attorneys, and respectfully submits her proposed voir dire questions pursuant to Rule 24(a) of the Federal Rules of Criminal Procedure. The Court is requested to pursue more detailed questioning if a particular juror's answer reveals that further inquiry is appropriate and, in such instance, to conclude with an inquiry as to whether the particular fact or circumstance would influence the juror in favor of or against the government or the defense.

Court's Introduction

Good morning to all of you. I want to just tell you, for those of you who have not been through this process before, we will be asking you some questions here. The purpose of the questions is not to be nosey, but just to allow me and also the attorneys in the case to make an informed decision about whether or not you could be fair and impartial as a juror in this particular case. After we ask you these questions, the lawyers in the case will have a certain number of what we call preemptory challenges that they can exercise, which will excuse some of you. Then some of you will remain as jurors, and those of you who remain will be the jurors who actually serve in this case. Let me explain to you just a little bit about what this case involves. This is a criminal case. There are five defendants. All defendants are charged in Count One with Conspiracy to Commit Securities Fraud and Wire Fraud. Defendant Dallas Hastie is further charged with Securities Fraud, Aggravated Currency Structuring, Money Laundering, and Wire Fraud. Defendant Paris Marshall is further charged with Securities Fraud and Wire Fraud. Defendant Louis Houston is further charged with Wire Fraud. Defendant Tokyo Murray is further charged with Money Laundering and Wire Fraud. Defendant Helsinki Robinson is not charged in any additional counts. The defendants have pleaded not guilty. And I should tell you that the indictment is not evidence of any kind against the defendants. It's just a mechanical means by which the case is brought to this court for trial here this morning. The defendants in the case, of course, as I will tell you later as well, begin with a clean slate, with no evidence at all against them.

Knowledge of the Case and Participants

1. Having heard that much about the case, has any member of this panel heard anything about this case prior to coming to court here today? Has any juror read, heard, or seen news media or other public reports concerning this case, including in newspapers or on the internet or otherwise? Raise your hand if you have.

2. Does any juror have any personal knowledge of the charges in the indictment in this case? If so, what is that personal knowledge? Will that personal knowledge cause you to feel that you cannot decide the fact issues of this case fairly and impartially?

3. Let me introduce to you some of the people who will be involved in the trial here. First, seated at the table closest to you, Assistant United States Attorney, Dan Hays. Other than perhaps having seen him here in court, does anybody know Mr. Hays? Next to Mr. Hays is Ms. Kate Whitworth, also an assistant U.S. attorney. Does anybody know Ms. Whitworth? Okay, Mr. Hays, would you please introduce your case agent and others seated at your table? Do any of you know, or have had any dealings, directly or indirectly, with the case agent, or anyone else seated at the government's table? Do you know any relative, friend, or associate of Mr. Hays, Ms. Whitworth, the case agent, or anyone seated at the government's table? Mr. Hays and Ms. Whitworth work for Tammy Dickinson, the U.S. Attorney for the Western District of Missouri. Does anyone know Ms. Dickinson or anyone who works for the U.S. Attorney's Office?

4. Marion Maughmer of Johnson, Smith, & Shook represents Ms. Marshall. Does anybody know Mr. Maughmer? Is anyone familiar with his law firm? Mr. Maughmer, please introduce your client and co-counsel. Do any of you know, or have had any dealings, directly

or indirectly, with the defendant or her counsel, or with any relative, friend, or associate of the defendant or her counsel? [Please repeat for each defense attorney and their client.]

5. I am U.S. District Judge Brian C. Kays. Does anyone know me or have had any dealings with me, my staff, or my family, directly or indirectly?

Background/Education/Employment

6. All of you have received a little list of questions. At this time, starting here with the first prospective juror, would you please, stand and tell us a little bit about yourself from the information that's requested there. [Please repeat with each prospective juror.]

7. Thank you all for that. That helps us get to know you, and I think saves time in the long run, so we don't have to ask some questions. You've heard what this case is about and what the allegations are. Is there anything about these allegations that would prevent any of you from being fair and impartial to both sides in this case? Raise your hand. And don't hesitate to do so if you have any feelings one way or another about this.

8. You'll be asked to make your decision in this case based just on the evidence that you hear in the courtroom. Will anybody not be able to do that?

9. You know just generally what the allegations are and who's involved here. Is there any reason why any member of the jury panel would not be able to be fair and impartial in this case to both sides, to the government and to each individual defendant? Raise your hand.

10. This case is expected to take ____ days to try. It's possible that it could be extended to ______ days, although we wouldn't be in court all that time, my best guess is the case should be able to be completed in three weeks. Does that present any particular scheduling problem for any member of this panel?

11. Have any of you taken undergraduate courses in criminal justice or attended law school? Do any of you have experience in criminal law? Do you have any legal training whatsoever including taking paralegal courses?

12. Does your spouse or a family member have experience in criminal law? If so, please state the general nature of that experience.

13. Have any of you, your close family or friends ever worked, either formally or informally, or applied for employment with, a law enforcement agency? By law enforcement agency, I mean organizations such as the Police Department, FBI, Circuit Attorney's or County Prosecutor's Office, the United States Attorney's Office, U.S. Department of Justice,

CIA, IRS, SEC, Secret Service, Military Police, GSA Guards, private security firms, and the like?

14. Have any of you, your close family or friends ever worked, either formally or informally, or applied for employment with, the U.S. Securities and Exchange Commission, FBI, or Missouri Secretary of State's Office? Does any juror have any bias or prejudice for or against the U.S. Attorney's Office, FBI, SEC, or Secretary of State's Office?

15. How many of you (or your close friends or relatives) have been employed by any prison, jail, department of corrections, probation office, or parole agency?

16. Have any of you (or your close friends or relatives) ever worked for a federal, state or local court system in any capacity?

17. Have any of you (or your close friends or relatives) ever worked for a brokerage company, mutual fund company, or securities company? Have you or any relatives worked on Wall Street? Have you or any family member worked for American Century, DST, or Waddell Reed?

Prior Jury/Litigation Experience

18. Has any member of the jury, a family member, or a close friend been involved in a criminal or civil trial at the state or federal level? If so, please give details. Were you/they satisfied with the outcome? Do you feel that the outcome was fair? Why or why not? What do you think of the job that your/their lawyer did? Did you serve as jury foreperson during trial? Is there anything about that experience that would affect your ability to sit as a juror in this case? Will you be able to put that past experience aside, consider the evidence in this case and apply the instructions the judge gives you in this case?

19. Has any jury member, or a family member, or a close friend ever had to testify in court or at a deposition? What were the circumstances? How did you/they feel about testifying?

20. Has any member of the jury had any unpleasant associations with lawyers, judges or the courts? If so, would that experience interfere with your ability to decide this case?

Nature of the Charges

21. During the trial, you will hear evidence regarding the securities industry. Does the fact that the charges involve the securities industry, investing, or fraud allegedly committed in connection with the securities industry make it difficult for any of you to render a fair verdict? As jurors in this case, you would be required to set aside your concerns and attitudes on general investment issues and decide this case independently

and solely on the evidence and the instructions as the Court gives them to you. How many of you feel that you might find that difficult?

22. For those of you who have invested in securities (such as stocks, bonds, options, etc.), will your experience as an investor affect your ability to be fair and impartial in this case? Are any of you accredited investors?

23. Have any of you worked in the securities industry? Have any of you served as a director or officer of a public- or privately-held company? Will your experience in that industry affect your ability to be fair and impartial to both the government and the defendants?

24. Do any of you believe that the securities industry should not be regulated by the state or federal government? Does any juror feel that you cannot decide fairly and impartially a case that involves allegations of securities fraud?

25. Is anyone here familiar with American Banking? Has any juror invested in American Banking? Is there anything about your knowledge of American Banking that would cause you to feel that you cannot decide fact issues of this case fairly and impartially?

26. Does any juror know, either directly or indirectly, the following individuals who may be called to testify as witnesses or whose names may come up during the trial? [The Court is requested to read the names listed on the government's witness list and defendants' witness lists.]

27. Has any juror or any close relative or friend ever been involved or appeared as a witness in any investigation by the SEC or Missouri Secretary of State's Office?

28. Have any of you formed any opinions about either the prosecutor or defense attorneys which would affect you in deciding this case?

29. How many of you feel that federal agent testimony is more likely to be believable or reliable than testimony by another witness?

30. If you had to choose who to believe, a federal agent or a witness called by a defendant, how many of you would be more likely to believe the federal agent because he or she is a federal agent?

31. How many of you agree that, in general, federal agents don't make mistakes?

32. How many of you have strong feelings about crime? Have you, a family member, or a close friend been a victim of a crime? Have you, a family member, or a close friend been a victim of financial fraud?

33. If the trial attracts local press attention, will each of you follow the court's instructions to refrain from viewing or reading any such reports in order to assure a fair trial based only on the evidence presented to you here in the courtroom?

34. Is there any member of the jury who does not wish to sit on this jury for any reason whatsoever? Does anyone have a reason that they would prefer not to sit, but wants to keep the reason private?

Presumption of Innocence and Burden of Proof

35. You will be instructed at the beginning and conclusion of trial that an indictment is simply an accusation. It is not evidence of anything. To the contrary, all defendants are presumed to be innocent. Thus each defendant, even though charged, begins the trial with no evidence against him or her. So the presumption of innocence alone is sufficient to find that each defendant is not guilty and can be overcome only if the government proves, beyond a reasonable doubt, each element of the crimes charged. Is there anyone here who feels that each of the defendants should be required to prove his or her innocence?

36. Does anyone feel that the defendants are probably guilty just based on the fact that they have been charged with these crimes?

37. Do you believe that a person can be falsely accused of a crime?

38. Have any of you ever been a victim, or know somebody who has been a victim, of a false allegation?

39. There is no burden on the defendants to prove their innocence. Thus, each individual defendant has the right not to testify. That is, each defendant can remain silent throughout this trial. Will any of you be disappointed if a defendant decides not to testify? Do any of you believe a defendant has an obligation to prove his or her innocence? Would any of you consider a defendant's failure to testify as evidence of guilt?

40. Some co-defendants have pleaded guilty to a crime which arose out of the same events for which these defendants are on trial. You cannot consider those guilty pleas as any evidence of these defendants' guilt. Would any of you feel that because others pleaded guilty in this case, that these defendants must also be guilty?

41. There are five defendants on trial. You must give separate consideration to the evidence about each individual. Each defendant is entitled to be treated separately. Would any of you have trouble considering, separately, each crime charged against each individual defendant?

42. You will receive instructions at the end of trial that each of you must make your own conscientious decision regarding guilt or innocence, but only after you have considered all the evidence, discussed it fully with your fellow jurors, and listened to the views of your fellow jurors. Will each of you agree to make up your own minds individually and return only a verdict to which you agree? Will any of you join a verdict just because the majority of the other jurors favor it, regardless of your personal belief as to the facts?

43. The government has the burden at trial to prove each and every element of the charges beyond a reasonable doubt. That burden is much higher than proof by preponderance of the evidence or "more likely than not," which is the standard in civil cases. Does anyone think that the government's burden of proof—beyond a reasonable doubt—is too high a standard or an unfair standard?

44. One of the issues in this case is whether defendants acted in good faith. Good faith is a complete defense to the charges of securities fraud and wire fraud. The essence of a good faith defense is that one who acts with honest intentions cannot be convicted of a crime requiring fraudulent intent. Will anyone have a problem finding that one or more of the defendants acted in good faith if the evidence warrants such a conclusion?

45. Is there anyone here who would hesitate to vote "not guilty" if the government fails to prove its case?

Dated: November 7, 2022

Respectfully Submitted,

JOHNSON, SMITH & SHOOK L.L.P.

By /s/ Russell K. Knox
Russell K. Knox #567892
Marion J. Maughmer #456214

10000 Highland Street
Jefferson City, Missouri 65101
Phone: (573) 980-0000
Fax: (573) 980-0001

ATTORNEYS FOR MS. MARSHALL

CERTIFICATE OF SERVICE

The undersigned hereby certifies that a copy of the foregoing was delivered on November 7, 2022, to the CM-ECF system of the United States District Court for the Western District of Missouri for electronic delivery to all counsel of record.

/s/ Russell K. Knox
Russell K. Knox #567892

IN THE UNITED STATES DISTRICT COURT FOR THE WESTERN DISTRICT OF MISSOURI CENTRAL DIVISION

UNITED STATES OF AMERICA,	)	
	)	
Plaintiff,	)	
	)	
v.	)	No. 20-cr-0501-BCK
	)	
	)	
PARIS MARSHALL,	)	
	)	
Defendant.	)	

MS. PARIS MARSHALL'S PROPOSED WITNESS LIST

COMES NOW Ms. Paris Marshall, by and through her attorneys, and submits her Proposed Witness List. Ms. Marshall reserves the right to seek leave of Court to amend this list and states that she may call the following witnesses at trial:

1. Ms. Paris Marshall, defendant;
2. Any and all experts noticed by Ms. Marshall;
3. All witnesses listed by the government; and
4. All witnesses listed by co-defendants (excluding co-defendants).

Dated: November 7, 2022

Respectfully Submitted,

JOHNSON, SMITH & SHOOK L.L.P.

By /s/ Russell K. Knox
Russell K. Knox #567892
Marion J. Maughmer #456214

10000 Highland Street
Jefferson City, Missouri 65101
Phone: (573) 980-0000
Fax: (573) 980-0001

ATTORNEYS FOR MS. MARSHALL

CERTIFICATE OF SERVICE

The undersigned hereby certifies that a copy of the foregoing was delivered on November 7, 2022, to the CM-ECF system of the United States District Court for the Western District of Missouri for electronic delivery to all counsel of record.

/s/ Russell K. Knox
Russell K. Knox #567892

IN THE UNITED STATES DISTRICT COURT FOR THE WESTERN DISTRICT OF MISSOURI CENTRAL DIVISION

UNITED STATES OF AMERICA,	)	
	)	
Plaintiff,	)	
	)	
v.	)	No. 20-cr-0501-BCK
	)	
	)	
PARIS MARSHALL,	)	
	)	
Defendant.	)	

MS. PARIS MARSHALL'S PROPOSED EXHIBIT LIST

COMES NOW Ms. Paris Marshall, by and through her attorneys, and submits this list of exhibits which she may offer in her case-in-chief during trial of this matter. Ms. Marshall reserves the right to seek leave of Court to amend this list with additional exhibits, should additional evidence be discovered prior to trial. Ms. Marshall also reserves the right to offer additional exhibits for impeachment during cross-examination of witnesses for the government, should such potential exhibits become relevant due to the presentation of government testimony and/or evidence.

Dated: November 7, 2022

Respectfully Submitted,

JOHNSON, SMITH & SHOOK L.L.P.

By /s/ Russell K. Knox
Russell K. Knox #567892
Marion J. Maughmer #456214

10000 Highland Street
Jefferson City, Missouri 65101
Phone: (573) 980-0000
Fax: (573) 980-0001

ATTORNEYS FOR MS. MARSHALL

CERTIFICATE OF SERVICE

The undersigned hereby certifies that a copy of the foregoing was delivered on November 7, 2022, to the CM-ECF system of the United States District Court for the Western District of Missouri for electronic delivery to all counsel of record.

/s/ Russell K. Knox
Russell K. Knox #567892

IN THE UNITED STATES DISTRICT COURT FOR THE WESTERN DISTRICT OF MISSOURI CENTRAL DIVISION

UNITED STATES OF AMERICA,	)	
	)	
Plaintiff,	)	
	)	
v.	)	No. 20-cr-0501-BCK
	)	
	)	
PARIS MARSHALL,	)	
	)	
Defendant.	)	

MS. PARIS MARSHALL'S PROPOSED EXHIBIT LIST

✓ = Offered & admitted without objection.

X. = Offered & admitted over objection.

Ex. = Offered but objected to and excluded.

N.O. = Marked but not offered.

D.B. = Admitted, de bene.

W.D. = Offered then withdrawn.

Ltd. = Admitted for limited purposes.

I hereby certify that I have this date ______________________________ received from the clerk, U.S. District Court, Western District of Missouri, the following numbered exhibits for which I will hold myself responsible.

____

Printed Name

____

Signature

[Insert Exhibit List]

IN THE UNITED STATES DISTRICT COURT FOR THE WESTERN DISTRICT OF MISSOURI CENTRAL DIVISION

UNITED STATES OF AMERICA,	)	
	)	
Plaintiff,	)	
	)	
v.	)	No. 20-cr-0501-BCK
	)	
	)	
PARIS MARSHALL,	)	
	)	
Defendant.	)	

MS. PARIS MARSHALL'S PROPOSED JURY INSTRUCTIONS

COMES NOW Ms. Paris Marshall, by and through her attorneys, and submits her attached proposed Jury Instructions. Ms. Marshall reserves the right to request and submit additional instructions.

Dated: November 7, 2022

Respectfully Submitted,

JOHNSON, SMITH & SHOOK L.L.P.

By /s/ Russell K. Knox
Russell K. Knox #567892
Marion J. Maughmer #456214

10000 Highland Street
Jefferson City, Missouri 65101
Phone: (573) 980-0000
Fax: (573) 980-0001

ATTORNEYS FOR MS. MARSHALL

CERTIFICATE OF SERVICE

The undersigned hereby certifies that a copy of the foregoing was delivered on November 7, 2022, to the CM-ECF system of the United States District Court for the Western District of Missouri for electronic delivery to all counsel of record.

/s/ Russell K. Knox

Russell K. Knox #567892

TABLE OF CONTENTS

Proposed Instruction No. 22	Reasonable Doubt
Proposed Instruction No. 23	Election of Foreperson; Duty to Deliberate; Punishment Not a Factor; Communications with Court; Cautionary; Verdict Form
Proposed Instruction No. 24	Venue
Proposed Instruction No. 25	Character and Reputation, for Truthfulness, Witnesses (Including the Defendant)
Proposed Instruction No. 26	Testimony under Grant of Immunity or Plea Bargain
Proposed Instruction No. 27	Testimony of Accomplice
Proposed Instruction No. 28	Credibility—Cooperating Witness
Proposed Instruction No. 29	Eyewitness Testimony
Proposed Instruction No. 30	Opinion Evidence—Expert Witness
Proposed Instruction No. 31	Conspiracy: Elements (18 U.S.C. § 371)
Proposed Instruction No. 32	Conspiracy: Elements (18 U.S.C. § 371) Explained
Proposed Instruction No. 33	Conspiracy: "Agreement" Explained
Proposed Instruction No. 34	Conspiracy: Co-Conspirator Acts and Statements
Proposed Instruction No. 35	Wire Fraud (18 U.S.C. § 1343)
Proposed Instruction No. 36	Securities Fraud (15 U.S.C. § 77Q(a), 15 U.S.C. § 78J(b), and 17 C.F.R. § 240.10b-5)
Proposed Instruction No. 37	Fraud—Puffery; Forward Looking Statements; Optimism
Proposed Instruction No. 38	Structuring Financial Transactions (31 U.S.C. §§ 5324(a)(3) and (d)(2))
Proposed Instruction No. 39	31 U.S.C. § 5324(a)(3) Definition of Structuring Financial Transactions
Proposed Instruction No. 40	Engaging in Monetary Transactions in Property Derived from Specified Unlawful Activity (18 U.S.C. § 1957)
Proposed Instruction No. 41	18 U.S.C. § 1957 Definitions
Proposed Instruction No. 42	Good Faith (Fraud Cases)
Proposed Instruction No. 43	Theory of the Defense—Paris Marshall Verdict Form

PRELIMINARY INSTRUCTIONS BEFORE OPENING STATEMENTS

INSTRUCTION NO. ______

Members of the Jury Panel, if you have a cell phone, smart phone, iPhone, Android device, or any other wireless communication device with you, please take it out now and turn it off. Do not turn it to vibration or silent; power it down. [During jury selection, you must leave it off.] (Pause for 30 seconds to allow them to comply, then tell them the following:)

If you are selected as a juror in this case, you cannot talk about the case or communicate with anyone else about the case until I tell you that such discussions are allowed. You cannot even discuss the case with your fellow jurors until I tell you to begin deliberations at the end of the trial. When I say you cannot communicate with anyone about the case in any way, this includes communications in writing, through email, via text messaging, on blogs, via comments, posts, or by accessing any social media websites and apps [give examples of currently popular social media applications, e.g., Twitter, Facebook, Instagram, LinkedIn, YouTube, WhatsApp, Snapchat, Tiktok, and NextDoor]. Similarly, you cannot post your own thoughts on any aspect of the trial. The point is that you must not access or allow any app or communication of any kind to expose you to outside information or opinions about this case, or to expose others to your opinions about the case, during the trial. Many of the tools you use to access email, social media, and the internet display third-party notifications, pop-ups, or ads while you are using them. These communications may be intended to persuade you or your community on an issue and could influence you in your service as a juror in this case. For example, while accessing your email, social media, or the internet, through no fault of your own, you might see pop-ups containing information about this case or the matters, legal principles, individuals or other entities involved in this case. [This means you will need to stay off all social media platforms for the duration of the trial.] These are only examples. The sole exception to this rule about communications will occur during deliberations, when I will direct you to discuss the case with the other jurors. If you feel that you cannot do this, then you cannot let yourself become a member of the jury in this case. Is there anyone who will not be able to comply with this restriction?

Throughout the trial, and even during deliberations, you also cannot conduct any type of independent or personal research or investigation regarding any matters related to this case. Therefore, you cannot use your cell phones, iPads, notebooks, tablets, computers or any other device to do any research or investigation regarding this case, the matters in the case, the legal issues in the case, or the individuals or other entities involved in the case. This includes accessing sites such as Google Maps, Google Earth, Casenet, PACER, or any other internet search engines. You must also ignore any and all information about the case you might see, even accidentally, while using your phone, browsing online, or accessing online or electronic apps. This prohibition is mandatory because you must base the decisions you will make in this case solely on what you hear and see in this courtroom. [If you feel that you cannot do this, then you cannot let yourself become a member of the jury in this case. Is there anyone who will not be able to comply with this restriction?]

I understand you may want to tell your family, close friends and other people about your participation in this trial so that you can explain when you are required to be in court. While you can tell them about these sort of logistical issues, you should warn them that you cannot speak about the details of the case and they should not ask you about this case, tell you anything they know or think they know about it, or discuss this case in your presence. If you discuss the case with someone other than the other jurors during deliberations, you may be influenced in your verdict by their opinions. That would not be fair to the parties, and it would result in a verdict that is not based on the evidence and the law.

The parties have a right to have this case decided only on evidence they know about and that has been presented here in court. If you do some research, investigation, or experiment that we don't know about, then your verdict may be influenced by inaccurate, incomplete, or misleading information that has not been tested by the trial process, including the oath to tell the truth and by cross-examination. Each of the parties is entitled to a fair trial, rendered by an impartial jury, and you must conduct yourself so as to maintain the integrity of the trial process. If you decide a case based on information not presented in court, you will have denied the parties a fair trial in accordance with the rules of this country and you will have done an injustice. It is very important that you abide by these rules. Failure to follow these instructions could result in the case having to be retried.

[If a violation of these rules results in unnecessary delays or a retrial, costs or contempt of Court penalties may be assessed to those responsible.]

[Are there any of you who cannot or will not abide by these rules concerning communication with others and outside research in any way, shape, or form during this trial?] (And then continue with other voir dire.)

[It is also important that you discharge your duties without discrimination, meaning that bias regarding the race, color, ethnicity, national origin, religion, gender, gender identity, sexual orientation, disability, or economic circumstances of the defendant, any witnesses, or other participant(s) associated with the trial should play no part in the exercise of your judgment throughout the trial.]

[Because personal opinions, biases, and other beliefs, whether conscious or unconscious, favorable or unfavorable, can affect your thoughts, how you remember, what you see and hear, whom you believe or disbelieve, and how you make important decisions, the attorneys may ask you some questions related to these issues. Your answers must not only be truthful, but they must be full and complete. Some biases we are aware or conscious of and others we might not be fully aware of, which is why they are called "implicit biases" or "unconscious biases." Unconscious biases are stereotypes, attitudes, or preferences that people may consciously reject but may express without conscious awareness, control, or intention. Like conscious bias, unconscious bias, too, can affect how we evaluate information and make decisions.]

[Are there any of you who cannot or will not abide by these rules concerning communication with others and outside research in any way, shape, or form during this trial?] (And then continue with other voir dire.)

I may not repeat these things to you before every recess but keep them in mind until you are discharged.

Ms. Marshall's Proposed Instruction No. 1

Instructions before Voir Dire

Eighth Circuit Model Jury Instructions (Criminal) § 0.01.

INSTRUCTION NO. ______

During this recess, and every other recess, do not discuss this case among yourselves or with anyone else, including your family and friends. Do not allow anyone to discuss the case with you or within your hearing. "Do not discuss" also means do not email, send text messages, blog, post on social media or engage in any other form of written, oral, or electronic communication, as I instructed you before.

Do not read anything about this case from any source, to include newspapers, Facebook, online, or via social media. Do not watch any televised account, to include online videos about this case. Do not listen to any radio program, podcasts, or other audio sources on the subject of this trial. Do not conduct any electronic research of any kind or consult with any other sources about this case, the people involved in the case, or its general subject matter. You must keep your mind open and free of all outside information of any kind. Only in this way will you be able to fulfill your duty to decide the case fairly, based solely on the evidence and my instructions on the law. If you decide this case on anything else, you will have done an injustice. It is very important that you follow these instructions.

The Sixth Amendment of our Constitution guarantees a trial by an impartial jury. This means that, as jurors, you must decide this case based solely on the evidence and law presented to you here in this courtroom. Until all the evidence and arguments have been presented and you begin to deliberate, you may not discuss this case with anyone, even your fellow jurors. After you start to deliberate, you may discuss the case, the evidence, and the law as it has been presented, but only with your fellow jurors. You cannot discuss it with anyone else until you have returned a verdict and the case has come to an end. I'll now walk through some specific examples of what this means.

First, this means that, during the trial, you must not conduct any independent research about this case, or the matters, legal issues, individuals, or other entities involved in this case. Just as you must not search or review any traditional sources of information about this case (such as dictionaries, reference materials, or television news or entertainment programs), you also must not access any electronic resources for information about this case, about the witnesses or parties involved, or about the legal issues raised during the case. For example, you cannot look up the meaning of an objection raised during the case. It is also improper to visit or view, including electronically, any place discussed in this case. The bottom line for the important work you will be doing is that you must base your verdict only on the evidence presented in this courtroom, along with instructions on the law that I will provide.

Second, this means that you must not communicate about the case with anyone. This includes your family and friends, until deliberations, when you will discuss the case with only other jurors. During deliberations, you must continue not to communicate about the case with anyone else. Most of us use smartphones, tablets, or computers in our daily lives to access the internet, for information, and to participate in social media platforms. To remain impartial jurors, however, you must not communicate with anyone about this case, whether in person, in writing, or through email, text messaging, blogs, or posts on social media websites and apps (such as Twitter, Facebook, Instagram, LinkedIn, YouTube, WhatsApp, Snapchat, Tiktok, and NextDoor).

Please note that these restrictions are intended to apply to all kinds of communications about this case, even those that are not directed at any particular person or group. Communications like blog posts or tweets can be shared to an ever-expanding circle of people and can have an unexpected impact on this trial. For example, a post you make to your social media account might ultimately be viewed by a witness who is not supposed to know what has happened in this courtroom before he or she has testified. For these reasons, you must inform me immediately if you learn about or share any information about the case outside of this courtroom, even if by accident, or if you discover that another juror has done so.

[Finally, a word about an even newer challenge for trials such as this one—persons, entities, and even foreign governments may seek to manipulate your opinions, or your impartiality during deliberations, using the communications I've already discussed or using fake social media accounts. But these misinformation efforts might also be undertaken through targeted advertising online or in social media. Many of the tools you use to access email, social media, and the internet display third-party notifications, pop-ups, or ads while you are using them. These communications may be intended to persuade you or your community on an issue and could influence you in your service as a juror in this case. For example, while accessing your email, social media, or the internet, through no fault of your own, you might see pop-ups containing information about this case or the matters, legal principles, individuals or other entities involved in this case. Please be aware of this possibility, ignore any pop-ups or ads that might be relevant to what we are doing here, and certainly do not click through to learn more if these notifications or ads appear. If this happens, you must let me know.]

Because it is so important to the parties' rights that you decide this case based solely on the evidence and my instructions on the law, at the beginning of each day, I may ask you whether you have learned about or shared any information outside of this courtroom. (I like to let the jury know in advance that I may be doing that, so you are prepared for the question.)

I hope that for all of you this case is interesting and noteworthy.

Ms. Marshall's Proposed Instruction No. 2

Instructions at End of Voir Dire

Eighth Circuit Model Jury Instructions (Criminal) § 0.02.

INSTRUCTION NO. ______

Ladies and gentlemen: I will take a few moments now to give you some initial instructions about this case and about your duties as jurors. At the end of the trial I will give you further instructions. I may also give you instructions during the trial. Unless I specifically tell you otherwise, all such instructions—both those I give you now and those I give you later—are equally binding on you and must be followed.

[Describe your court's policy, such as "You must leave your cell phone, smart phone, iPhone, and any other wireless communication devices in the jury room during the trial and may only use them during breaks. However, you are not allowed to have cell phones in the jury room during your deliberations. You may give the cell phone to the [bailiff] [deputy clerk] for safekeeping just before you start to deliberate. It will be returned to you when your deliberations are complete."]

This is a criminal case, brought against the defendants by the United States Government. Dallas Hastie is charged with Conspiracy, Aggravated Currency, Structuring, Securities Fraud, Money Laundering, and Wire Fraud. Paris Marshall is charged with Conspiracy, Securities Fraud, and Wire Fraud. Louis Houston is charged with Conspiracy and Wire Fraud. Tokyo Murray is charged with Conspiracy, Money Laundering, and Wire Fraud. Helsinki Robinson is charged with Conspiracy. Those charges are set forth in what is called an indictment, which I will summarize as follows: All of the defendants did knowingly, willfully, and with intent to defraud, conspire and agree amongst themselves to commit the crimes of Securities Fraud and Wire Fraud with the objective of obtaining money through the fraudulent sale of stock in American Banking Corp. This fraud was perpetrated by Mr. Hastie, Ms. Marshall, Mr. Houston, and Ms. Murray making fraudulent material misrepresentations and omissions to investors and concealing the conspirators' individual compensation. In furtherance of the conspiracy and as a result of the conspiracy, Mr. Hastie and Ms. Murray did knowingly engage in monetary transactions in interstate commerce worth more than $10,000 with money derived from the unlawful activity of wire fraud. Additionally, Mr. Hastie did knowingly and willingly structure transactions or assist in the structuring of transactions with domestic financial institutions to evade reporting or recordkeeping requirements under federal law.

You should understand that an indictment is simply an accusation. It is not evidence of anything. The defendants have pleaded not guilty and are presumed to be innocent unless and until proved guilty beyond a reasonable doubt.

It will be your duty to decide from the evidence whether each defendant is guilty or not guilty of the crimes charged. From the evidence, you will decide what the facts are. You are entitled to consider that evidence in the light of your own observations and experiences in the affairs of life. You may use reason and common sense to draw deductions or conclusions from facts which have been established by the evidence. You will then apply those facts to the law which I give you in these and in my other instructions, and in that way reach your verdict. You are the sole judges of the facts, but you must follow my instructions, whether you agree with them or not. You have taken an oath to do so.

Do not allow sympathy or prejudice to influence you. The law demands of you a just verdict, unaffected by anything except the evidence, your common sense, and the law as I give it to you.

You should not take anything I may say or do during the trial as indicating what I think of the evidence or what I think your verdict should be.

Finally, please remember that only these defendants, not anyone else, are on trial here, and that these defendants are on trial only for the crimes charged, not for anything else.

Ms. Marshall's Proposed Instruction No. 3

General: Nature of Case; Nature of Indictment; Burden of Proof; Presumption of Innocence; Duty of Jury; Cautionary

Eighth Circuit Model Jury Instructions (Criminal) § 1.01.

INSTRUCTION NO. ______

In order to help you follow the evidence, I will now give you a brief summary of the elements of the crimes charged, which the government must prove beyond a reasonable doubt to make its case:

Conspiracy

One, on or before September 1, 2018, two or more people reached an agreement to commit the crimes of Securities Fraud and Wire Fraud with the objective of obtaining money through the fraudulent sale of stock in American Banking Corp.;

Two, the defendant voluntarily and intentionally joined in the agreement, either at the time it was first reached or at some later time while it was still in effect;

Three, at the time the defendant joined in the agreement, the defendant knew the purpose of the agreement or understanding; and

Four, while the agreement was in effect, a person or persons who had joined in the agreement knowingly did an act for the purpose of carrying out or carrying forward the agreement.

Wire Fraud

One, the defendant voluntarily and intentionally devised or participated in a scheme to defraud, obtaining money by means of material false representations or promises;

Two, the defendant did so with the intent to defraud; and

Three, the defendant used, or caused to be used, an interstate wire communication, in furtherance of, or in an attempt to carry out, some essential step in the scheme.

Securities Fraud

One, in connection with the offer or sale of the securities, the stock in American Banking Corp., the defendant, directly or through others:

(a) employed a device or scheme to defraud; or

(b) obtained money or property by means of any untrue statement of a material fact; or

(c) engaged in a transaction, practice, or course of business that operated, or would operate, as a fraud or deceit upon any person;

Two, the defendant acted knowingly, voluntarily, and intentionally, and with the intent to defraud; and

Three, the defendant made use of interstate commerce, in furtherance of this conduct.

Aggravated Structuring

One, the defendant had knowledge that the financial institution is required to report currency transactions in amounts greater than $10,000;

Two, the defendant structured a currency transaction for the purpose of evading this reporting requirement;

Three, the transaction involved one or more domestic financial institutions; and

Four, the defendant participated in a pattern of illegal activity including more than $100,000 in a 12-month period.

Money Laundering

One, the defendants knowingly engaged in a monetary transaction;

Two, the monetary transaction was of a value greater than $10,000 derived from a criminal offense;

Three, the defendants then knew that the monetary transaction involved proceeds of a criminal offense;

Four, the monetary transaction took place in the Western District of Missouri; and

Five, the monetary transaction in some way or degree affected interstate commerce.

You should understand, however, that what I have just given you is only a preliminary outline. At the end of the trial I will give you a final instruction on these matters. If there is any difference between what I just told you, and what I tell you in the instructions I give you at the end of the trial, the instructions given at the end of the trial must govern you.

Ms. Marshall's Proposed Instruction No. 4

Elements of the Offense — Preliminary

Eighth Circuit Model Jury Instructions (Criminal) § 1.02.

INSTRUCTION NO. ______

I have mentioned the word "evidence." "Evidence" includes the testimony of witnesses, documents and other things received as exhibits, any facts that have been stipulated—that is, formally agreed to by the parties and any facts that have been judicially noticed—that is, facts which I say you may, but are not required to, accept as true, even without evidence.

Certain things are not evidence. I will list those things for you now:

1. Statements, arguments, questions, and comments by lawyers representing the parties in the case are not evidence.

2. Objections are not evidence. Lawyers have a right to object when they believe something is improper. You should not be influenced by the objection. If I sustain an objection to a question, you must ignore the question and must not try to guess what the answer might have been.

3. Testimony that I strike from the record, or tell you to disregard, is not evidence and must not be considered.

4. Anything you see or hear about this case outside the courtroom is not evidence, unless I specifically tell you otherwise during the trial.

Furthermore, a particular item of evidence is sometimes received for a limited purpose only. That is, it can be used by you only for one particular purpose, and not for any other purpose. I will tell you when that occurs and instruct you on the purposes for which the item can and cannot be used.

Finally, some of you may have heard the terms "direct evidence" and "circumstantial evidence." You are instructed that you should not be concerned with those terms. The law makes no distinction between direct and circumstantial evidence. You should give all evidence the weight and value you believe it is entitled to receive.

Ms. Marshall's Proposed Instruction No. 5

Evidence Limitations

Eighth Circuit Model Jury Instructions (Criminal) §§ 1.03, 5.06, 6.18; see 2B Fed. Jury Prac. & Instr. § 62:03 (6th ed.); 21A Sec. Crimes Appendix 87.

INSTRUCTION NO. ______

In deciding what the facts are, you may have to decide what testimony you believe and what testimony you do not believe. You may believe all of what a witness said, or only part of it, or none of it.

[In deciding what testimony of any witness to believe, consider the witness's intelligence, the opportunity the witness had to have seen or heard the things testified about, the witness's memory, any motives that the witness may have for testifying a certain way, the manner of the witness while testifying, whether that witness said something different at an earlier time, the general reasonableness of the testimony, and the extent to which the testimony is consistent with other evidence that you believe].

[Again you must avoid bias, conscious or unconscious, based on a witness's race, color, ethnicity, national origin, religion, gender, gender identity, sexual orientation, disability, or economic circumstances in your determination(s) of credibility.]

Ms. Marshall's Proposed Instruction No. 6

Credibility of Witnesses

Eighth Circuit Model Jury Instructions (Criminal) § 1.05.

INSTRUCTION NO. ______

At the end of the trial you must make your decision based on what you recall of the evidence. You will not have a written transcript to consult, and it may not be practical for the court reporter to read back lengthy testimony. You must pay close attention to the testimony as it is given.

[If you wish, however, you may take notes to help you remember what witnesses said. If you do take notes, please keep them to yourself until you and your fellow jurors go to the jury room to decide the case. And do not let note-taking distract you so that you do not hear other answers by the witness.

[When you leave at night, your notes will be secured and not read by anyone.]

Ms. Marshall's Proposed Instruction No. 7

No Transcript Available—Note Taking

Eighth Circuit Model Jury Instructions (Criminal) § 1.06A.

INSTRUCTION NO. _____

When attorneys have finished their examination of a witness, you may ask questions of the witness (describe procedure to be used here). If the rules of evidence do not permit a particular question, I will so advise you. Following your questions, if any, the attorneys may ask additional questions.

Ms. Marshall's Proposed Instruction No. 8

Questions by Jurors

Eighth Circuit Model Jury Instructions (Criminal) § 1.06B.

INSTRUCTION NO. ______

During the trial it may be necessary for me to talk with the lawyers out of the hearing of the jury, either by having a bench conference here while the jury is present in the courtroom or by calling a recess. Please understand that while you are waiting, we are working. The purpose of these conferences is to decide how certain evidence is to be treated under the rules of evidence, and to avoid confusion and error. We will, of course, do what we can to keep the number and length of these conferences to a minimum.

Ms. Marshall's Proposed Instruction No. 9

Bench Conferences and Recesses

Eighth Circuit Model Jury Instructions (Criminal) § 1.07.

INSTRUCTION NO. ______

To ensure fairness, you as jurors must obey the following rules:

First, do not talk or communicate among yourselves about this case, or about anyone involved with it, until the end of the case when you go to the jury room to decide on your verdict.

Second, do not talk with anyone else about this case, or about anyone involved with it, until the trial has ended, and you have been discharged as jurors.

Third, when you are outside the courtroom do not let anyone tell you anything about the case, or about anyone involved with it [until the trial has ended, and your verdict has been accepted by me]. If someone should try to talk to you about the case [during the trial], please report it to the [bailiff] [deputy clerk]. (Describe person.)

Fourth, during the trial you should not talk with or speak to any of the parties, lawyers or witnesses involved in this case—you should not even pass the time of day with any of them. It is important not only that you do justice in this case, but that you also give the appearance of doing justice. If a person from one side of the lawsuit sees you talking to a person from the other side—even if it is simply to pass the time of day—an unwarranted and unnecessary suspicion about your fairness might be aroused. If any lawyer, party, or witness does not speak to you when you pass in the hall, ride the elevator or the like, it is because they are not supposed to talk to or visit with you.

Fifth, it may be necessary for you to tell your family, close friends, teachers, coworkers, or employer about your participation in this trial. You can explain when you are required to be in court and can warn them not to ask you about this case, tell you anything they know or think they know about this case, or discuss this case in your presence. You must not communicate with anyone or post information about the parties, witnesses, participants, [claims] [charges], evidence, or anything else related to this case. You must not tell anyone anything about the jury's deliberations in this case until after I accept your verdict or until I give you specific permission to do so. If you discuss the case with someone other than the other jurors during deliberations, it could create the perception that you have clearly decided the case or that you may be influenced in your verdict by their opinions. That would not be fair to the parties, and it may result in the verdict being thrown out and the case having to be retried. During the trial, while you are in the courthouse and after you leave for the day, do not provide any information to anyone by any means about this case. Thus, for example, do not talk face-to-face or use any electronic device or media, such as the telephone, a cell or smart phone, computer, any online service, any text or instant messaging service, any internet chat room, blog, or website such as Facebook, Tiktok, Instagram, YouTube, Twitter, or any other way to communicate to anyone any information about this case until I accept your verdict.

Sixth, do not do any research—on the internet, via electronic devices, in libraries, in the newspapers, or in any other way—or make any investigation about this case on your own. Do not visit or view any place discussed in this case and do not use any computerized devices or phones to electronically search online for or to view any place discussed in the testimony. Also, do not research any information about this case, the law, or the people involved, including the parties, the witnesses, the lawyers, or the judge.

Seventh, do not read anything about this case, whether it is a news story, an article in print, something online, something on social media, or in any blog or app about the case or about anyone involved with it, or listen to any radio, television, online, video, or other types of reports about the case or about anyone involved with it. [In fact, until the trial is over, I suggest that you avoid reading any news at all, and avoid listening to any broadcasts of any kind, to include electronic kinds such as podcasts. I do not know whether there might be any news reports of this case, but if there are, you might inadvertently find yourself reading or listening to something before you could do anything about it. If you want, you can have your spouse or a friend clip out any stories for you to look at after the trial is over.] I can assure you, however, that by the time you have heard the evidence in this case, you will know what you need to return a just verdict.

The parties have a right to have the case decided only on evidence they know about and that has been introduced here in court. If you do some research or investigation or experiment that we don't know about, then your verdict may be influenced by inaccurate, incomplete, or misleading information that has not been tested by the trial process, including the oath to tell the truth and by cross-examination. All of the parties are entitled to a fair trial, rendered by an impartial jury, and you must conduct yourself so as to maintain the integrity of the trial process. If you decide a case based on information not presented in court, you will have denied the parties a fair trial in accordance with the rules of this country and you will have done an injustice. It is very important that you abide by these rules. Remember, you have taken an oath to abide by these rules and you must do so. [Failure to follow these instructions may result in the case having to be retried and could result in you being held in contempt.]

Eighth, do not make up your mind during the trial about what the verdict should be. Keep an open mind until after you have gone to the jury room to decide the case and you and your fellow jurors have discussed the evidence.

Ninth, faithful performance by you of your duties as jurors is vital to the administration of justice. You should perform your duties without prejudice or fear, and solely from a fair and impartial consideration of the whole case.

[Our system of justice depends on jurors like you being able and willing to make careful and fair decisions. A first response is often like a reflex; it may be quick and automatic. Even though a quick response may not be the result of conscious thought, it may influence how we judge people or even how we remember or evaluate evidence. You must not decide this case based on personal likes or dislikes, sympathy, prejudice, fear, public opinion, or biases, including unconscious biases such as stereotypes, attitudes, or preferences that people may consciously reject but may express without conscious awareness, control, or intention. Take the time to reflect carefully and consciously about the evidence.]

Ms. Marshall's Proposed Instruction No. 10

Conduct of the Jury

Eighth Circuit Model Jury Instructions (Criminal) § 1.08.

INSTRUCTION NO. ______

The trial will proceed in the following manner:

First, the government will make an opening statement. [Next the defendant's attorney may, but does not have to, make an opening statement.] An opening statement is not evidence but is simply a summary of what the attorney expects the evidence to be.

The government will then present its evidence, and counsel for the defendant may cross examine. Following the government's case, the defendant may, but does not have to, present evidence, testify, or call other witnesses. If the defendant calls witnesses, the government may cross-examine them.

After presentation of evidence is completed, the attorneys will make their closing arguments to summarize and interpret the evidence for you. As with opening statements, closing arguments are not evidence. The court will instruct you further on the law. After that you will retire to deliberate on your verdict.

Ms. Marshall's Proposed Instruction No. 11

Outline of Trial

Eighth Circuit Model Jury Instructions (Criminal) § 1.09.

INSTRUCTIONS FOR USE DURING TRIAL

INSTRUCTION NO. ______

During this recess, and every other recess, you must not discuss this case with anyone, including the other jurors, members of your family, people involved in the trial, or anyone else. Do not allow anyone to discuss the case with you or within your hearing. Only you have been chosen as jurors in this case, and only you have sworn to uphold the law—no one else has been chosen to do this. You should not even talk among yourselves about the case before you have heard all the evidence and the case has been submitted to you by me for deliberations, because it may affect your final decision. If anyone tries to talk to you about the case, please let me know about it immediately.

When I say "you must not discuss the case with anyone," I also mean do not email, send text messages, blog, or engage in any other form of written, oral, or electronic communication, as I instructed you before.

[Do not read any newspaper or other written account, watch any televised account, or listen to any radio program about this trial. Do not conduct any electronic research or consult with any other sources about this case, the people involved in the case, or its general subject matter. You must keep your mind open and free of outside information. Only in this way will you be able to decide the case fairly, based solely on the testimony, evidence presented in this courtroom, and my instructions on the law. If you decide this case on anything else, you will have done an injustice. It would be a violation of your oath for you to base your decision on someone else's view or opinion, or upon other information you acquire outside the courtroom. It is very important that you follow these instructions.]

I may not repeat these things to you before every recess, but keep them in mind throughout the trial.

Ms. Marshall's Proposed Instruction No. 12

Duties of Jury—Recesses

Eighth Circuit Model Jury Instructions (Criminal) § 2.01.

INSTRUCTION NO. _____

You are about to hear recordings of conversations. These conversations were legally recorded, and you may consider the recordings just like any other evidence.

Ms. Marshall's Proposed Instruction No. 13

Wiretap or Other Recorded Evidence

Eighth Circuit Model Jury Instructions (Criminal) § 2.05.

INSTRUCTION NO. _____

You have heard testimony that [the defendant] made a statement to (name of person or agency). It is for you to decide:

First, whether [the defendant] made the statement; and

Second, if so, how much weight you should give to it.

In making these two decisions, you should consider all of the evidence, including the circumstances under which the statement may have been made.

Ms. Marshall's Proposed Instruction No. 14

Statement by Defendant

Eighth Circuit Model Jury Instructions (Criminal) § 2.07.

INSTRUCTION NO. _____

As you know, there are five defendants on trial here: Dallas Hastie, Paris Marshall, Tokyo Murray, Louis Houston, and Helsinki Robinson. Each defendant is entitled to have his or her case decided solely on the evidence which applies to him or her. You may consider some of the evidence in this case only against defendant (name); you may not consider that evidence against the other defendants.

You may consider the [evidence] [testimony] [exhibit] you [are about to hear] [just heard about], (describe testimony or exhibit), only against defendant (name). You must not consider that evidence when you are deciding if the government has proved, beyond a reasonable doubt, its case against defendant[s] (name[s]).

Ms. Marshall's Proposed Instruction No. 15

Evidence Admitted Against Only One Defendant

Eighth Circuit Model Jury Instructions (Criminal) § 2.14.

INSTRUCTION NO. ______

You may consider the statement of defendant (name) only in the case against [him] [her], and not against the other defendants. You may not consider or discuss defendant (name)'s statement in any way when you are deciding if the government proved, beyond a reasonable doubt, its case against the other defendants.

Ms. Marshall's Proposed Instruction No. 16

Statement of One Defendant in Multi-Defendant Trial

Eighth Circuit Model Jury Instructions (Criminal) § 2.15.

FINAL INSTRUCTIONS

INSTRUCTION NO. ______

Members of the jury, the instructions I gave you at the beginning of the trial and during the trial remain in effect. I now give you some additional instructions.

You must, of course, continue to follow the instructions I gave you earlier, as well as those I give you now. You must not single out some instructions and ignore others, because all are important. [This is true even though some of those I gave you [at the beginning of] [during] trial are not repeated here.]

[The instructions I am about to give you now [as well as those I gave you earlier] are in writing and will be available to you in the jury room.] [I emphasize, however, that this does not mean they are more important than my earlier instructions. Again, *all* instructions, whenever given and whether in writing or not, must be followed.]

Ms. Marshall's Proposed Instruction No. 17

Introduction

Eighth Circuit Model Jury Instructions (Criminal) § 3.01.

INSTRUCTION NO. ______

It is your duty to find from the evidence what the facts are. You will then apply the law, as I give it to you, to those facts. You must follow my instructions on the law, even if you thought the law was different or should be different.

[You should not be influenced by any person's race, color, ethnicity, national origin, religion, gender, gender identity, sexual orientation, disability, or economic circumstances. You must decide the case solely on the evidence and the law before you and must not be influenced by any personal likes or dislikes, opinions, prejudices, sympathy, or biases, including unconscious bias. Unconscious biases are stereotypes, attitudes, or preferences that people may consciously reject but may express without conscious awareness, control, or intention. Like conscious bias, unconscious bias, too, can affect how we evaluate information and make decisions.

The law demands of you a just verdict, unaffected by anything except the evidence, your common sense, and the law as I give it to you.

Ms. Marshall's Proposed Instruction No. 18

Duty of Jury

Eighth Circuit Model Jury Instructions (Criminal) § 3.02.

INSTRUCTION NO. ______

I have mentioned the word "evidence." The "evidence" in this case consists of the testimony of witnesses, the documents and other things received as exhibits, and the facts that have been stipulated—this is, formally agreed to by the parties.

You may use reason and common sense to draw deductions or conclusions from facts which have been established by the evidence in the case.

Certain things are not evidence. I will list those things again for you now:

1. Statements, arguments, questions, and comments by lawyers representing the parties in the case are not evidence.
2. Objections are not evidence. Lawyers have a right to object when they believe something is improper. You should not be influenced by the objection. If I sustained an objection to a question, you must ignore the question and must not try to guess what the answer might have been.
3. Testimony that I struck from the record, or told you to disregard, is not evidence and must not be considered.
4. Anything you saw or heard about this case outside the courtroom is not evidence.

Finally, if you were instructed that some evidence was received for a limited purpose only, you must follow that instruction.

Ms. Marshall's Proposed Instruction No. 19

Evidence; Limitations

Eighth Circuit Model Jury Instructions (Criminal) § 3.03.

INSTRUCTION NO. ______

In deciding what the facts are, you may have to decide what testimony you believe and what testimony you do not believe. You may believe all of what a witness said, or only part of it, or none of it.

In deciding what testimony to believe, consider the witness's intelligence, the opportunity the witness had to have seen or heard the things testified about, the witness's memory, any motives that witness may have for testifying a certain way, the manner of the witness while testifying, whether that witness said something different at an earlier time, the general reasonableness of the testimony, and the extent to which the testimony is consistent with any evidence that you believe.

In deciding whether or not to believe a witness, keep in mind that people sometimes hear or see things differently and sometimes forget things. You need to consider therefore whether a contradiction is an innocent misrecollection or lapse of memory or an intentional falsehood, and that may depend on whether it has to do with an important fact or only a small detail.

You should judge the testimony of the defendant in the same manner as you judge the testimony of any other witness.

Ms. Marshall's Proposed Instruction No. 20

Credibility of Witnesses

Eighth Circuit Model Jury Instructions (Criminal) § 3.04.

INSTRUCTION NO. ______

The Indictment in this case charges the defendants with seventeen different crimes.

Count One charges that all of the defendants committed the crime of Conspiracy.

Count Two charges that Mr. Hastie and Ms. Marshall committed the crime of Securities Fraud.

Count Three charges that Mr. Hastie committed the crime of Aggravated Currency Structuring.

Count Four charges that Mr. Hastie committed the crime of Money Laundering.

Count Five charges Mr. Murray committed the crime of Money Laundering.

Counts Seven through Eight charge that Mr. Hastie committed the crime of Wire Fraud.

Counts Nine through Fourteen charge that Ms. Marshall committed the crime of Wire Fraud.

Counts Fifteen through Sixteen charge that Mr. Houston committed the crime of Wire Fraud.

Count Seventeen charges that Mr. Murray committed the crime of Wire Fraud. Each defendant has pleaded not guilty to each of those charges.

The Indictment is simply the document that formally charges the defendants with the crimes for which they are on trial. The Indictment is not evidence. At the beginning of the trial, I instructed you that you must presume each defendant to be innocent. Thus, the defendants began the trial with a clean slate, with no evidence against them.

The presumption of innocence alone is sufficient to find each defendant not guilty of each count. This presumption can be overcome as to each charge only if the government proved during the trial, beyond a reasonable doubt, each element of that charge.

Keep in mind that you must give separate consideration to the evidence about each individual defendant. Each defendant is entitled to be treated separately, and you must return a separate verdict for each defendant. Also keep in mind that you must consider, separately, each crime charged against each individual defendant, and you must return a separate verdict for each of those crimes charged.

There is no burden upon a defendant to prove that he or she is innocent. Instead, the burden of proof remains on the government throughout the trial. The fact that a defendant did not testify must not be considered by you in any way, or even discussed, in arriving at your verdict.

Ms. Marshall's Proposed Instruction No. 21

Description of Charges; Indictment Not Evidence; Presumption of Innocence; Burden of Proof (Multiple Defendants, Multiple Counts)

Eighth Circuit Model Jury Instructions (Criminal) § 3.08.

INSTRUCTION NO. _____

Reasonable doubt is doubt based upon reason and common sense, and not doubt based on speculation. A reasonable doubt may arise from careful and impartial consideration of all the evidence or from a lack of evidence. Proof beyond a reasonable doubt is proof of such a convincing character that a reasonable person, after careful consideration, would not hesitate to rely and act upon that proof in life's most important decisions. Proof beyond a reasonable doubt is proof that leaves you firmly convinced of the defendant's guilt. Proof beyond a reasonable doubt does not mean proof beyond all possible doubt.

Ms. Marshall's Proposed Instruction No. 22

Reasonable Doubt

Eighth Circuit Model Jury Instructions (Criminal) § 3.11.

INSTRUCTION NO. ______

In conducting your deliberations and returning your verdict, there are certain rules you must follow. I will list those rules for you now.

First, when you go to the jury room, you must select one of your members as your foreperson. That person will preside over your discussions and speak for you here in court.

Second, it is your duty, as jurors, to discuss this case with one another in the jury room. You should try to reach agreement if you can do so without violence to individual judgment, because a verdict—whether guilty or not guilty—must be unanimous.

Each of you must make your own conscientious decision, but only after you have considered all the evidence, discussed it fully with your fellow jurors, and listened to the views of your fellow jurors.

Do not be afraid to change your opinions if the discussion persuades you that you should. But do not come to a decision simply because other jurors think it is right, or simply to reach a verdict.

Third, if the defendant is found guilty, the sentence to be imposed is my responsibility. You may not consider punishment in any way in deciding whether the government has proved its case beyond a reasonable doubt.

Fourth, if you need to communicate with me during your deliberations, you may send a note to me through the marshal or bailiff, signed by one or more jurors. I will respond as soon as possible either in writing or orally in open court. Remember that you should not tell anyone—including me—how your votes stand numerically.

Fifth, your verdict must be based solely on the evidence and on the law which I have given to you in my instructions. The verdict whether guilty or not guilty must be unanimous. Nothing I have said or done is intended to suggest what your verdict should be—that is entirely for you to decide.

Finally, the verdict form is simply the written notice of the decision that you reach in this case. [The form reads: (read form)]. You will take this form to the jury room, and when each of you has agreed on the verdict[s], your foreperson will fill in the form, sign and date it, and advise the marshal or bailiff that you are ready to return to the courtroom.

[If more than one form was furnished, you will bring the unused forms in with you.]

Ms. Marshall's Proposed Instruction No. 23

Election of Foreperson; Duty to Deliberate; Punishment Not a Factor; Communications with Court; Cautionary; Verdict Form

Eighth Circuit Model Jury Instructions (Criminal) § 3.12.

INSTRUCTION NO. ______

The government must prove it is more likely true than not true that the offense charged was begun, continued or completed in the Western District of Missouri. I instruct you that the Western District of Missouri encompasses the western half of the state of Missouri and includes the cities of Kansas City, Jefferson City, Springfield, Joplin, and St. Joseph. You decide these facts by considering all of the evidence and deciding what evidence is more believable. This is a lower standard than proof beyond a reasonable doubt. The requirement of proof beyond a reasonable doubt applies to all other issues in the case.

Ms. Marshall's Proposed Instruction No. 24

Venue

Eighth Circuit Model Jury Instructions (Criminal) § 3.13.

INSTRUCTION NO. ______

You have heard testimony about the character and reputation of [(name of witness)] [the defendant] [defendant (name)] for truthfulness. You may consider this evidence only in deciding whether to believe the testimony of [(name of witness)] [the defendant] [defendant (name)] and how much weight to give to it.

Ms. Marshall's Proposed Instruction No. 25

Character and Reputation, for Truthfulness, Witnesses (Including the Defendant)

Eighth Circuit Model Jury Instructions (Criminal) § 4.02.

INSTRUCTION NO. ______

You have heard evidence that (name of witness) has made a plea agreement with the government. [His] [Her] testimony was received in evidence and may be considered by you. You may give [his] [her] testimony such weight as you think it deserves. Whether or not [his] [her] testimony may have been influenced by the plea agreement is for you to determine.

The witness's guilty plea cannot be considered by you as any evidence of this defendant's guilt. The witness's guilty plea can be considered by you only for the purpose of determining how much, if at all, to rely upon the witness's testimony.

Ms. Marshall's Proposed Instruction No. 26

Testimony under Grant of Immunity or Plea Bargain

Eighth Circuit Model Jury Instructions (Criminal) § 4.04.

INSTRUCTION NO. ______

You have heard testimony from (name of witness) who stated that [he] [she] participated in the crime charged against the defendant. [His] [Her] testimony was received in evidence and may be considered by you. You may give [his] [her] testimony such weight as you think it deserves. Whether or not [his] [her] testimony may have been influenced by [his] [her] desire to please the government or to strike a good bargain with the government about [his] [her] own situation is for you to determine.

Ms. Marshall's Proposed Instruction No. 27

Testimony of Accomplice

Eighth Circuit Model Jury Instructions (Criminal) § 4.05A.

INSTRUCTION NO. ______

You [have heard] [are about to hear] evidence that [name of witness] hopes to receive a reduced sentence on criminal charges pending against [him] [her] in return for [his] [her] cooperation with the government in this case. [Name of witness] entered into an agreement with [name of agency] which provides (specify general agreement, for example, that in return for his assistance, the government will dismiss certain charges, recommend a less severe sentence [which could be less than the mandatory minimum sentence for the crime[s] with which he/she is charged]). [[Name of witness] is subject to a mandatory minimum sentence, that is, a sentence that the law provides must be of a certain minimum length. If the prosecutor handling this witness's case believes [he] [she] provided substantial assistance, that prosecutor can file in the court in which the charges are pending against this witness a motion to reduce [his] [her] sentence below the statutory minimum. The judge has no power to reduce a sentence for substantial assistance unless the Government, acting through the United States Attorney, files such a motion. If such a motion for reduction of sentence for substantial assistance is filed by the government, then it is up to the judge to decide whether to reduce the sentence at all, and if so, how much to reduce it.]

You may give the testimony of this witness such weight as you think it deserves. Whether or not testimony of a witness may have been influenced by [his] [her] hope of receiving a reduced sentence is for you to decide.

Ms. Marshall's Proposed Instruction No. 28

Credibility—Cooperating Witness

Eighth Circuit Model Jury Instructions (Criminal) § 4.05B.

INSTRUCTION NO. ______

The value of identification testimony depends on the opportunity the witness had to observe the offender at the time of the offense and to make a reliable identification later. Eyewitness identification must be evaluated with particular care.

In evaluating such testimony, you should consider all of the factors mentioned in these instructions concerning your assessment of the credibility of any witness, and you should also consider, in particular, whether the witness had an adequate opportunity to observe the person in question at the time of the offense and whether the identification is reliable. You may consider, in that regard, such matters as the witness's eyesight and ability to observe the person in question under the circumstances, the length of time the witness had to observe the person in question, the prevailing conditions at that time in terms of lighting, visibility or distance and the like, whether the witness had known or observed the person at earlier times, and any description provided by the witness after the event and before identifying the defendant. Factors that bear on the likelihood of misidentification include the passage of time between the witness's exposure to the person in question and identification of the defendant, whether the witness was under stress when [he] [she] first encountered the person in question, whether the person in question carried a weapon, and the race of the person in question and the witness.

[In general, a witness uses his or her senses to make an identification. Usually, the witness identifies an offender by the sense of sight—but this is not necessarily so, and other senses may be used.]

You should also consider whether the identification made by the witness after the offense was the product of [his] [her] own recollection. You may consider, in that regard, the strength of the identification and the circumstances under which the identification was made, keeping in mind that a witness may be certain but mistaken.

[You may also take into account that an identification made by picking the defendant out of a group of similar individuals is generally more reliable than one which results from the presentation of the defendant alone to the witness. In that regard, you may consider whether the identification was made [in a live or photographic lineup. In determining the reliability of the lineup, you should consider whether the makeup of the lineup suggested to the witness who should be selected. You should consider the procedures used by law enforcement in conducting the lineup and whether those procedures affected the reliability of the witness's identification.] [in a live or photographic show up.

A "show up" is a procedure in which law enforcement presents an eyewitness with a single suspect for identification. In determining the reliability of the identification made at the "show up," you may consider such factors as the time elapsed between the witness's opportunity to view the person in question and the "show up," instructions given to the witness during the "show up" procedure, and any other circumstances which may affect the reliability of the identification.]]

If the identification by the witness may have been influenced by the circumstances under which the defendant was presented to [him] [her] for identification, you should scrutinize the identification with great care.

[You may take into account any occasions in which the witness failed to make an identification of the defendant, or made an identification that was inconsistent with [his] [her] identification at trial.] The government has the burden of proving identity beyond a reasonable doubt. It is not essential that the witness be free from doubt as to the correctness of the identification. However, you, the jury, must be satisfied beyond a reasonable doubt of the accuracy of the identification of the defendant before you may find [him] [her] guilty. If you are not convinced beyond a reasonable doubt that the defendant was the person who committed the crime, you must find the defendant not guilty.

Ms. Marshall's Proposed Instruction No. 29

Eyewitness Testimony

Eighth Circuit Model Jury Instructions (Criminal) § 4.08.

INSTRUCTION NO. ______

You have heard testimony from persons described as experts. Persons who, by knowledge, skill, training, education, or experience, have become expert in some field may state their opinions on matters in that field and may also state the reasons for their opinion.

Expert testimony should be considered just like any other testimony. You may accept or reject it, and give it as much weight as you think it deserves, considering the witness's education and experience, the soundness of the reasons given for the opinion, the acceptability of the methods used, and all the other evidence in the case.

Ms. Marshall's Proposed Instruction No. 30

Opinion Evidence—Expert Witness

Eighth Circuit Model Jury Instructions (Criminal) § 4.10.

INSTRUCTION NO. ______

It is a crime for two or more people to agree to commit a crime. The crime of conspiracy, as charged in Count One of the indictment, has four elements:

One, on or before September 1, 2018, two or more people reached an agreement to commit the crimes of securities fraud and wire fraud with the objective of obtaining money through the fraudulent sale of stock in American Banking Corp.;

Two, the defendant voluntarily and intentionally joined in the agreement, either at the time it was first reached or at some later time while it was still in effect;

Three, at the time the defendant joined in the agreement, the defendant knew the purpose of the agreement or understanding; and

Four, while the agreement was in effect, a person or persons who had joined in the agreement knowingly did one or more acts for the purpose of carrying out or carrying forward the agreement.

If all of these elements have been proved beyond a reasonable doubt as to the defendant, then you must find the defendant guilty of the crime charged under Count One; otherwise you must find the defendant not guilty of this crime under Count One.

Ms. Marshall's Proposed Instruction No. 31

Conspiracy: Elements (18 U.S.C. § 371)

Eighth Circuit Model Jury Instructions (Criminal) § 5.06A-1.

INSTRUCTION NO. ______

Element One -

Element One requires that two [or more] people reached an agreement to commit the crimes of securities fraud and wire fraud with the objective of obtaining money through the fraudulent sale of stock in American Banking Corp.

The indictment charges a conspiracy to commit securities fraud and wire fraud. For you to find that the government has proved a conspiracy, you must unanimously find that there was an agreement to act with the objective of obtaining money through the fraudulent sale of stock in American Banking Corp. [You must unanimously agree which purpose or purposes motivated the members of the agreement to act. If you are unable to unanimously agree on at least one of these purposes, you cannot find the defendant guilty of conspiracy].

[The agreement between two or more people to commit the crimes of securities fraud and wire fraud does not need to be a formal agreement or be in writing. A verbal or oral understanding can be sufficient to establish an agreement.]

[It does not matter whether the crimes of securities fraud and wire fraud were actually committed or whether the alleged participants in agreement actually succeeded in accomplishing their unlawful plan.]

[The agreement may last a long time or a short time. The members of an agreement do not all have to join it at the same time. You may find that someone joined the agreement even if you find that person did not know all of the details of the agreement.]

[A person may be a member of the agreement even if the person does not know all of the other members of the agreement or the person agreed to play only a minor part in the agreement.]

Element Two -

Element Two requires that the defendant voluntarily and intentionally joined the agreement.

If you have determined that two or more people reached an agreement to commit securities fraud and wire fraud, you must next decide whether the defendant voluntarily and intentionally joined that agreement, either at the time it was first formed or at some later time while it was still in effect.

Earlier, in deciding whether two or more people reached an agreement to commit the crimes of securities fraud and wire fraud, you could consider the acts and statements of each person alleged to be part of the agreement. Now, in deciding whether a defendant joined the agreement, you may consider only the acts and statements of that defendant.

[A person joins an agreement to commit securities fraud and wire fraud by voluntarily and intentionally participating in the unlawful plan with the intent to further the crimes of securities fraud and wire fraud.] [It is not necessary for you to find that the defendant knew all the details of the unlawful plan.]

[It is not necessary for you to find that the defendant reached an agreement with every person you determine was a participant in the agreement.]

[Evidence that a person was present at the scene of an event, or acted in the same way as others or associated with others, does not, alone, prove that the person joined a conspiracy. A person who has no knowledge of a conspiracy, but who happens to act in a way that advances the purpose of the conspiracy, does not thereby become a member. A person's mere knowledge of the existence of a conspiracy, or mere knowledge that an objective of a conspiracy was being considered or attempted, or mere approval of the purpose of a conspiracy, is not enough to prove that the person joined in a conspiracy.]

[The agreement may last a long time or a short time. The members of an agreement do not all have to join it at the same time. You may find that the defendant joined the agreement even if you find that the defendant did not know all of the details of the agreement.]

[A person may be a member of the agreement even if the person does not know all of the other members of the agreement or the person agreed to play only a minor part in the agreement.]

[To help you decide whether the defendant agreed to commit the crime of securities fraud, you should consider the elements of that crime, which are the following:

1. In connection with the offer or sale of the securities, the stock in American Banking Corp., the defendant, directly or through others:

    a. employed a device or scheme to defraud; or
    b. obtained money or property by means of any untrue statement of a material fact; or
    c. engaged in a transaction, practice, or course of business that operated, or would operate, as a fraud or deceit upon any person;

2. The defendant acted knowingly, voluntarily and intentionally, and with the intent to defraud; and
3. The defendant made use of interstate commerce, in furtherance of this conduct.

To help you decide whether the defendant agreed to commit the crime of wire fraud, you should consider the elements of that crime, which are the following:

1. The defendant voluntarily and intentionally devised or participated in a scheme to defraud, obtaining money by means of material false representations or promises;
2. The defendant did so with the intent to defraud; and
3. The defendant used, or caused to be used, an interstate wire communication, in furtherance of, or in an attempt to carry out, some essential step in the scheme.

You may consider these elements in determining whether the defendant agreed to commit the crimes of securities fraud and wire fraud, keeping in mind that this count of the indictment only charges a conspiracy to commit securities fraud and wire fraud, and does not charge that securities fraud and wire fraud were committed.

Element Three –

Element Three requires that the defendant knew the purpose of the agreement at the time the defendant joined the agreement.

A person knows the purpose of the agreement if [he] [she] is aware of the agreement and does not participate in it through ignorance, mistake, carelessness, negligence, or accident. It is seldom, if ever, possible to determine directly what was in the defendant's mind. Thus, the defendant's knowledge of the agreement and its purpose can be proved like anything else, from reasonable conclusions drawn from the evidence.

It is not enough that the defendant and other alleged participants in the agreement to commit the crimes of securities fraud or wire fraud simply met, discussed matters of common interest, acted in similar ways, or perhaps helped one another. The defendant must have known of the existence and purpose of the agreement. Without such knowledge, the defendant cannot be guilty of conspiracy, even if [his] [her] acts furthered the conspiracy.

Element Four –

Element Four requires that one of the persons who joined the agreement took some act for the purpose of carrying out or carrying forward the agreement.

The defendant does not have to personally commit an act in furtherance of the agreement, know about it, or witness it. It makes no difference which of the participants in the agreement did the act. This is because a conspiracy is a kind of "partnership," so that under the law each member is an agent or partner of every other member and each member is bound by or responsible for the acts of every other member done to further their scheme.

[The act done in furtherance of the agreement does not have to be an unlawful act. The act may be perfectly innocent in itself.]

[It is not necessary that the government prove that more than one act was done in furtherance of the agreement. It is sufficient if the government proves one such act; but in that event, in order to return a verdict of guilty, you must all agree which act was done.]

Ms. Marshall's Proposed Instruction No. 32

Conspiracy: Elements (18 U.S.C. § 371) Explained

Eighth Circuit Model Jury Instructions (Criminal) § 5.06A-2.

INSTRUCTION NO. ______

The Indictment charges that the defendants were members of a conspiracy to commit the crimes of securities fraud and wire fraud with the objective of obtaining money through the fraudulent sale of stock in American Banking Corp.

One of the issues you must decide is whether there were really two separate conspiracies—one among all the defendants to commit the crime of securities fraud, and another one among all the defendants to commit the crime of wire fraud.

The Government must convince you beyond a reasonable doubt that each defendant was a member of the conspiracy to commit the crimes of securities fraud or wire fraud, as charged in the indictment. If the Government fails to prove this as to a defendant, then you must find that defendant not guilty of the conspiracy charge, even if you find that [he] [she] was a member of some other conspiracy. Proof that a defendant was a member of some other conspiracy is not enough to convict.

But proof that a defendant was a member of some other conspiracy would not prevent you from returning a guilty verdict, if the Government also proved that [he] [she] was a member of the conspiracy to commit the crime of securities fraud or wire fraud with the objective of obtaining money through the fraudulent sale of stock in American Banking Corp., as charged in the indictment.

[A single conspiracy may exist even if all the members did not know each other, or never met together, or did not know what roles all the other members played. And a single conspiracy may exist even if different members joined at different times, or the membership of the group changed. Similarly, just because there were different subgroups operating in different places, or many different criminal acts committed over a long period of time, does not necessarily mean that there was more than one conspiracy. These are factors you may consider in determining whether more than one conspiracy existed.]

Ms. Marshall's Proposed Instruction No. 33

Conspiracy: "Agreement" Explained

Eighth Circuit Model Jury Instructions (Criminal) § 5.06B.

INSTRUCTION NO. ______

If you determined that an agreement existed and the defendant joined the agreement, then acts and statements knowingly done or made by a member of the agreement during the existence of the agreement and in furtherance of it, may be considered by you as evidence pertaining to the defendant, even though the acts and statements were done or made in the absence of and without the knowledge of the defendant. This includes acts done or statements made before the defendant joined the agreement, because a person who knowingly, voluntarily and intentionally joins an existing conspiracy becomes responsible for all of the conduct of the co-conspirators from the beginning of the conspiracy.

[Acts and statements which are made before the conspiracy began or after it ended are admissible only against the person making them and should not be considered by you against any other defendant.]

Ms. Marshall's Proposed Instruction No. 34

Conspiracy: Co-Conspirator Acts and Statements

Eighth Circuit Model Jury Instructions (Criminal) § 5.06D.

INSTRUCTION NO. ______

The crime of wire fraud as Mr. Hastie, Ms. Marshall, Mr. Houston, and Mr. Murray are each charged with in Counts Seven through Seventeen of the Indictment, has three elements:

One, the defendant voluntarily and intentionally devised or participated in a scheme to defraud, obtaining money by means of material false representations or promises;

Two, the defendant did so with the intent to defraud; and

Three, the defendant used, or caused to be used, an interstate wire communication, in furtherance of, or in an attempt to carry out, some essential step in the scheme.

The phrase "scheme to defraud" includes any plan or course of action intended to deceive or cheat another out of money by employing material falsehoods. It also means the obtaining of money from another by means of material false representations or promises. A scheme to defraud need not be fraudulent on its face but must include some sort of fraudulent misrepresentation or promise reasonably calculated to deceive a reasonable person.

A statement or representation is "false" when it is untrue when made or effectively conceals or omits a material fact.

A fact or representation is "material" if it has a natural tendency to influence, or is capable of influencing, the decision of a reasonable person in deciding whether to engage or not to engage in a particular transaction. However, whether a fact or representation is "material" does not depend on whether the person was actually deceived.

To act with "intent to defraud" means to act knowingly and with the intent to deceive someone for the purpose of causing some financial loss to another or bringing about some financial gain to oneself or another to the detriment of a third party. With respect to false statements, the defendant must have known the statement was untrue when made or have made the statement with reckless indifference to its truth or falsity.

It is not necessary that the use of the interstate wire communication by the participants themselves be contemplated or that the defendant actually uses an interstate wire communication or specifically intended that an interstate wire communication be used. It is sufficient if an interstate wire communication was in fact used to carry out the scheme and the use of an interstate wire communication by someone was reasonably foreseeable.

If you find from your consideration of all the evidence that the Government has proved each of these elements beyond a reasonable doubt as to the charge you are considering, then you should find the defendant guilty of that charge.

If, on the other hand, you find from your consideration of all the evidence that the Government has failed to prove any one of these elements beyond a reasonable doubt as to the charge you are considering, then you should find the defendant not guilty of that charge.

Ms. Marshall's Proposed Instruction No. 35

Wire Fraud (18 U.S.C. § 1343)

Eighth Circuit Model Jury Instructions (Criminal) § 6.18.1343; 18 U.S.C. § 1343.

INSTRUCTION NO. ______

The crime of securities fraud, as Mr. Hastie and Ms. Marshall are charged with in Count Two of the Indictment, has three elements:

One, in connection with the offer or sale of the securities, the stock in American Banking Corp., the defendant, directly or through others:

(a) employed a device or scheme to defraud; or

(b) obtained money or property by means of any untrue statement of a material fact; or

(c) engaged in a transaction, practice, or course of business that operated, or would operate, as a fraud or deceit upon any person;

Two, the defendant acted knowingly, voluntarily, and intentionally, and with the intent to defraud; and

Three, the defendant made use of interstate commerce, in furtherance of this conduct.

The phrase "scheme to defraud" includes any plan or course of action intended to deceive or cheat another out of money by employing material falsehoods. It also means the obtaining of money from another by means of material false representations or promises. A scheme to defraud need not be fraudulent on its face but must include some sort of fraudulent misrepresentation or promise reasonably calculated to deceive a reasonable person.

There is no requirement that the defendant was involved in the scheme from its inception, played a major role in the scheme, or had contact with the investors or purchasers of the securities in question. Nor is it necessary that the defendant was the actual seller or offeror of the securities. It is sufficient if only one person conceived the scheme and the defendant participated in the scheme or fraudulent conduct that involved the offer or sale of securities. Specifically, it is not necessary that the defendant personally made any untrue statement of, or failed to state, a material fact. It is sufficient if the defendant caused the statement to be made or the fact to be omitted.

A fact is "material" if it has a natural tendency to influence, or is capable of influencing, the decision of a reasonable person in deciding whether to engage or not to engage in a particular transaction; for example, if the fact could reasonably be expected to cause or induce a person to invest or to cause or to induce a person not to invest. However, whether a fact is "material" does not depend on whether the person was actually deceived. It does not matter whether the intended victims were gullible buyers or sophisticated investors because the securities laws protect gullible and unsophisticated investors as well as experienced investors.

It does not matter whether the alleged unlawful scheme was successful or not, or that the defendant profited or received any benefits as a result of the alleged scheme. Success is not an element of the crime charged. However, if you find that the defendant did profit from the alleged scheme, you may consider that in connection with Element Three, including intent to defraud, which will now be described.

To act with "intent to defraud" means to act knowingly and with the intent to deceive someone for the purpose of causing some financial loss to another or bringing about some financial gain to oneself or another to the detriment of a third party. With respect to false statements, the defendant must have known the statement was untrue when made or caused the statement to be made with reckless indifference to its truth or falsity.

The phrase "interstate commerce" means commerce in securities or any transportation or communication relating to securities between any combination of states, territories, and possessions of the United States, including the District of Columbia, or between any foreign country and any state, territory, or possession of the United States, including the District of Columbia. The term "commerce" includes, among other things, travel, trade, transportation, and communication. The internet is a means or instrument of communication in interstate commerce.

It is not necessary that the use of a means or instrumentality of interstate commerce by the participants themselves be contemplated or that the defendant personally use a means or instrumentality of interstate commerce, or specifically intended that a means or instrumentality of interstate commerce be used. It is sufficient if a means or instrumentality of interstate commerce were in fact used to carry out the scheme and such use by someone was reasonably foreseeable.

If you find from your consideration of all the evidence that the Government has proved each of these elements beyond a reasonable doubt as to the charge you are considering, then you should find the defendant guilty of that charge.

If, on the other hand, you find from your consideration of all the evidence that the Government has failed to prove any one of these elements beyond a reasonable doubt as to the charge you are considering, then you should find the defendant not guilty of that charge.

Ms. Marshall's Proposed Instruction No. 36

Securities Fraud (15 U.S.C. § 77Q(a), 15 U.S.C. § 78J(b), and 17 C.F.R. § 240.10b-5)

Eighth Circuit Model Jury Instructions (Criminal) § 6.15.77q(a) and 78j(b).

INSTRUCTION NO. ______

Even if a statement is untrue or misleading, it is not material and cannot support a charge of securities fraud if it constitutes puffery or sales talk that no reasonable investor would consider important in deciding whether to invest in American Banking Corp. People in charge of an enterprise are not required to take a gloomy, fearful or defeatist view of the future; subject to what current data indicates, they can be expected to be confident about their stewardship and the prospects of the business that they manage. For that reason, marketing pitches, expressions of general optimism, self-praise, and similar corporate cheerleading may be immaterial because they qualify as mere puffery, the type of superlatives that are common in business, and therefore are not the type of statements upon which an investor would rely.

Statements of mere belief or disbelief in current or future events, not accompanied by objective evidence that the statement also expressly or impliedly asserted something false or misleading about its subject matter, are not material as a matter of law, because no one would reasonably rely on another person's ability to predict the future.

Ms. Marshall's Proposed Instruction No. 37

Fraud—Puffery; Forward Looking Statements; Optimism

***In re Medtronic Inc., Sec. Litig.*, 618 F. Supp. 2d 1016, 1031 (D. Minn. 2009), and *aff'd sub nom. Detroit Gen. Ret. Sys. v. Medtronic, Inc.*, 621 F.3d 800 (8th Cir. 2010) (quoting *Novak v. Kasaks*, 216 F.3d 300, 315 (2d Cir. 2000)) ("[S]tatements containing simple economic projections, expressions of optimism, and other puffery are insufficient" to establish securities fraud."). *See also In re Target Corp. Sec. Litig.*, 955 F.3d 738, 743 n.2 (8th Cir. 2020) ("[S]tatements like 'we feel really good about where we are today[,]' are inactionable puffery . . . [or] 'optimistic statements' that cannot be 'supported by objective data or otherwise subject to verification by proof.'") (citation omitted).**

INSTRUCTION NO. _____

The crime of aggravated currency structuring, as Mr. Hastie is charged with in Count Three of the Indictment has four elements:

1. Mr. Hastie had knowledge that Amherst Credit Union is required to report currency transactions in amounts greater than $10,000;

2. Mr. Hastie structured a currency transaction for the purpose of evading this reporting requirement;

3. The transaction involved one or more domestic financial institutions.

I will define some of these terms in a moment; and

4. Mr. Hastie participated in a pattern of illegal activity including more than $100,000 in a 12-month period.

If you find from your consideration of all the evidence that the Government has proved each of these elements beyond a reasonable doubt as to the charge you are considering, then you should find the defendant guilty of that charge.

If, on the other hand, you find from your consideration of all the evidence that the Government has failed to prove any one of these elements beyond a reasonable doubt as to the charge you are considering, then you should find the defendant not guilty of that charge.

Ms. Marshall's Proposed Instruction No. 38

Structuring Financial Transactions (31 U.S.C. §§ 5324(a)(3) and (d)(2))

***See* Pattern Criminal Jury Instructions of the Seventh Circuit, 1072 (2022 Ed.); 31 U.S.C. §§ 5324(a)(3) and (d)(2).**

INSTRUCTION NO. ______

A financial institution must file a currency transaction report with the Internal Revenue Service every time a customer engages in a currency transaction of more than $10,000.00.

Credit unions are financial institutions.

A currency transaction is the physical transfer of currency from one person or entity to another person or entity.

A person structures a currency transaction when he conducts one or more currency transactions at one financial institution, on one or more days, with the purpose of evading currency transaction reporting requirements. Structuring may include breaking down a single sum of currency over $10,000 into smaller sums, or conducting a series of cash transactions all at or below $10,000, with the purpose of evading currency transaction reporting requirements.

You may find Mr. Hastie guilty of unlawfully structuring a transaction regardless of whether the financial institution filed a true and accurate currency transaction report.

Ms. Marshall's Proposed Instruction No. 39

31 U.S.C. § 5324(a)(3) Definition of Structuring Financial Transactions

Pattern Criminal Jury Instructions of the Seventh Circuit, 1074 (2022 Ed.).

INSTRUCTION NO. ______

The crime of engaging in a monetary transaction in property derived from Wire Fraud, as Mr. Hastie and Mr. Murray are charged with in Counts Seven through Eight and Seventeen of the Indictment, has five elements, which are:

The government must prove beyond a reasonable doubt each of the six following elements, which are:

One, the defendants knowingly engaged in a monetary transaction;

Two, the monetary transaction was of a value greater than $10,000 derived from Wire Fraud;

Three, the defendants then knew that the monetary transaction involved proceeds of a criminal offense;

Four, the monetary transaction took place in the Western District of Missouri; and

Five, the monetary transaction in some way or degree affected interstate commerce.

If you find from your consideration of all the evidence that the Government has proved each of these elements beyond a reasonable doubt as to the charge you are considering, then you should find the defendant guilty of that charge.

If, on the other hand, you find from your consideration of all the evidence that the Government has failed to prove any one of these elements beyond a reasonable doubt as to the charge you are considering, then you should find the defendant not guilty of that charge.

Ms. Marshall's Proposed Instruction No. 40

Engaging in Monetary Transactions in Property Derived from Specified Unlawful Activity (18 U.S.C. § 1957)

Eighth Circuit Model Jury Instructions (Criminal) § 6.18.1957; Pattern Criminal Jury Instructions of the Seventh Circuit, 812 (2022 Ed.).

INSTRUCTION NO. ______

The term "monetary transaction" means the deposit, withdrawal, transfer, or exchange, in or affecting interstate commerce, of funds or a monetary instrument, by, through, or to a financial institution.

"Interstate commerce" means trade, transactions, transportation, or communication between any point in a state and any place outside that state or between two points within a state through a place outside the state.

The term "financial institution" includes [commercial banks, trust companies, businesses engaged in vehicle sales including automobile sales, and businesses and persons engaged in real estate closings or settlements.]

The term "criminally derived property" means any property constituting, or derived from, proceeds obtained from a criminal offense.

Ms. Marshall's Proposed Instruction No. 41

18 U.S.C. § 1957 Definitions

Pattern Criminal Jury Instructions of the Seventh Circuit, 814 (2022 Ed.).

INSTRUCTION NO. ______

One of the issues in this case is whether the defendant acted in good faith. Good faith is a complete defense to the crimes of securities fraud and wire fraud if the defendant did not act with the intent to defraud, which is an element of the charge. The essence of the good faith defense is that one who acts with honest intentions cannot be convicted of a crime requiring fraudulent intent.

Good faith includes, among other things, an opinion or belief that is honestly held, even if the opinion is in error or the belief is mistaken. However, even though a defendant honestly held a certain opinion or belief (such as a belief that a business venture would ultimately succeed, that investors would make a profit, or that investors would not lose money), a defendant does not act in good faith if he or she also knowingly made false or fraudulent representations or promises, or otherwise acted with the intent to defraud or deceive another. Proof of fraudulent intent requires more than proof that a defendant only made a mistake in judgment or management, or was careless.

The Government has the burden of proving beyond a reasonable doubt that the defendant acted with the intent to defraud. Evidence that the defendant acted in good faith may be considered by you, together with all the other evidence, in determining whether or not the defendant acted with the intent to defraud.

Ms. Marshall's Proposed Instruction No. 42

Good Faith (Fraud Cases)

Eighth Circuit Model Jury Instructions (Criminal) § 9.08A.

INSTRUCTION NO. ______

Ms. Marshall has pled not guilty to all counts of this Indictment. I have instructed you that the burden of proof rests on the government to prove every element of each count beyond a reasonable doubt. Ms. Marshall's defense is that she never conspired to commit fraud or securities law violations, or any of the other alleged offenses of the conspiracy; and that she never committed any of the substantive offenses alleged, or aided or abetted in the commission of those offenses.

Specifically, by Ms. Marshall's plea of "not guilty," Ms. Marshall has denied knowledge of any of the alleged misconduct about which you have heard testimony. If you believe that the government has not proven beyond a reasonable doubt that Ms. Marshall had knowledge of the fraud and willfully participated in it, then you must acquit. Ms. Marshall could be aware of some of the conduct but not necessarily have enough knowledge or fully understand the implications of that knowledge sufficiently for you to conclude that she acted willfully. Remember that I have also instructed you that just because someone's conduct appears to assist or advance some illegal act does not, by itself, mean that the defendant was acting knowingly and willfully as the law requires.

In determining whether Ms. Marshall had such a good faith belief, you may consider—but are not bound by—whether other individuals involved in American Banking Corp. also believed that the statements were accurate. In determining whether Ms. Marshall knew or could have known these statements were inaccurate, you may consider—but are not bound by—whether other individuals with the means, the skills, and the responsibility of Ms. Marshall failed to detect the inaccuracies.

You must remember that by presenting a defense and pointing out evidence that Ms. Marshall has not assumed any burden of proof. Throughout the trial the burden of proof remains on the government. However, you can consider the defense presented by Ms. Marshall, along with all of the other evidence in deciding if the government has proven its case beyond a reasonable doubt.

Ms. Marshall's Proposed Instruction No. 43

Theory of the Defense—Paris Marshall

21A Sec. Crimes Appendix 87.

IN THE UNITED STATES DISTRICT COURT FOR THE WESTERN DISTRICT OF MISSOURI CENTRAL DIVISION

UNITED STATES OF AMERICA,	)	
	)	
Plaintiff,	)	
	)	
v.	)	No. 20-cr-0501-BCK
	)	
	)	
PARIS MARSHALL,	)	
	)	
Defendant.	)	

VERDICT FORM

COUNT ONE

We, the jury, find the defendant DALLAS HASTIE (not guilty/guilty) ______________________ of the crime of conspiracy to commit Securities Fraud and Wire Fraud with the objective of obtaining money through the fraudulent sale of stock in American Banking Corp. under Instruction No. ____.

We, the jury, find the defendant PARIS MARSHALL (not guilty/guilty) ___________________________ of the crime of conspiracy to commit Securities Fraud and Wire Fraud with the objective of obtaining money through the fraudulent sale of stock in American Banking Corp. under Instruction No. ____.

We, the jury, find the defendant LOUIS HOUSTON (not guilty/guilty) ___________________________ of the crime of conspiracy to commit Securities Fraud and Wire Fraud with the objective of obtaining money through the fraudulent sale of stock in American Banking Corp. under Instruction No. ____.

We, the jury, find the defendant TOKYO MURRAY (not guilty/guilty) ______________________ of the crime of conspiracy to commit Securities Fraud and Wire Fraud with the objective of obtaining money through the fraudulent sale of stock in American Banking Corp. under Instruction No. ____.

We, the jury, find the defendant HELSINKI ROBINSON (not guilty/guilty) ______________________ of the crime of conspiracy to commit Securities Fraud and Wire Fraud with the objective of obtaining money through the fraudulent sale of stock in American Banking Corp. under Instruction No. ____.

COUNT TWO

We, the jury, find the defendant DALLAS HASTIE (not guilty/guilty) ______________________ of the crime of Securities Fraud as charged in Count Two of the Indictment under Instruction No. ____.

We, the jury, find the defendant PARIS MARSHALL (not guilty/guilty) ______________________ of the crime of Securities Fraud as charged in Count Two of the Indictment under Instruction No. ____.

COUNT THREE

We, the jury, find the defendant DALLAS HASTIE (not guilty/guilty) __________________________ of the crime of Aggravated Currency Structuring as charged in Count Three of the Indictment under Instruction No. ____.

COUNT FOUR

We, the jury, find the defendant DALLAS HASTIE (not guilty/guilty) ______________________ of the crime of Money Laundering as charged in Count Four of the Indictment under Instruction No. ____.

COUNT FIVE

We, the jury, find the defendant TOKYO MURRAY (not guilty/guilty) ______________________ of the crime of Money Laundering as charged in Count Five of the Indictment under Instruction No. ____.

COUNT SEVEN

We, the jury, find the defendant DALLAS HASTIE (not guilty/guilty) ______________________ of the crime of Wire Fraud as charged in Count Seven of the Indictment under Instruction No. ____.

COUNT EIGHT

We, the jury, find the defendant DALLAS HASTIE (not guilty/guilty) ______________________ of the crime of Wire Fraud as charged in Count Eight of the Indictment under Instruction No. ____.

COUNT NINE

We, the jury, find the defendant PARIS MARSHALL (not guilty/ guilty) ____________________ of the crime of Wire Fraud as charged in Count Nine of the Indictment under Instruction No. ____.

COUNT TEN

We, the jury, find the defendant PARIS MARSHALL (not guilty/ guilty) ____________________ of the crime of Wire Fraud as charged in Count Ten of the Indictment under Instruction No. ____.

COUNT ELEVEN

We, the jury, find the defendant PARIS MARSHALL (not guilty/ guilty) ____________________ of the crime of Wire Fraud as charged in Count Eleven of the Indictment under Instruction No. ____.

COUNT TWELVE

We, the jury, find the defendant PARIS MARSHALL (not guilty/ guilty) ____________________ of the crime of Wire Fraud as charged in Count Twelve of the Indictment under Instruction No. ____.

COUNT THIRTEEN

We, the jury, find the defendant PARIS MARSHALL (not guilty/ guilty) ____________________ of the crime of Wire Fraud as charged in Count Thirteen of the Indictment under Instruction No. ____.

COUNT FOURTEEN

We, the jury, find the defendant PARIS MARSHALL (not guilty/ guilty) ____________________ of the crime of Wire Fraud as charged in Count Fourteen of the Indictment under Instruction No. ____.

COUNT FIFTEEN

We, the jury, find the defendant LOUIS HOUSTON (not guilty/ guilty) ____________________ of the crime of Wire Fraud as charged in Count Fifteen of the Indictment under Instruction No. ____.

COUNT SIXTEEN

We, the jury, find the defendant LOUIS HOUSTON (not guilty/ guilty) ____________________ of the crime of Wire Fraud as charged in Count Sixteen of the Indictment under Instruction No. ____.

COUNT SEVENTEEN

We, the jury, find the defendant TOKYO MURRAY (not guilty/guilty) ______________________ of the crime of Wire Fraud as charged in Count Seventeen of the Indictment under Instruction No. ____.

____

FOREPERSON OF THE JURY

DATE: __________________

Tab 3 Government's Proposed

**IN THE UNITED STATES DISTRICT COURT FOR THE
WESTERN DISTRICT OF MISSOURI
CENTRAL DIVISION**

UNITED STATES OF AMERICA,	)	
	)	
Plaintiff,	)	
	)	
v.	)	No. 20-cr-0501-BCK
	)	
	)	
PARIS MARSHALL,	)	
	)	
Defendant.	)	

GOVERNMENT'S PROPOSED VOIR DIRE QUESTIONS

COMES NOW the United States of America, by and through John F. Biden, United States Attorney, and Daniel W. Hays and Kathleen D. Whitworth, Assistant United States Attorneys, all for the Western District of Missouri, and files with this Honorable Court proposed voir dire questions to be asked the panel of prospective jurors.

1. Please have each juror state the following information:

(a) Name;
(b) Address;
(c) Marital status;
(d) Employment;
(e) Spouse's employment;
(f) County where the juror lives;
(g) Organizations to which the juror belongs; and
(h) Nature of formal education and last full year of school completed.

2. The government is represented by Daniel W. Hays and Kathleen D. Whitworth, Assistant United States Attorneys here in the Western District of Missouri. Does anyone here know them or the United States Attorney, John F. Biden, or any other member of the United States Attorney's Office? Various Special Agents of the Federal Bureau of

Investigation and Secret Service will be assisting prosecutors in the presentation of this case. Does anyone know [list special agents]? Does anyone know the defendants [list defendants]? Does anyone know the attorneys participating in this trial [list]?

3. The offices of the United States Attorney are located in Kansas City, Springfield, and Jefferson City, Missouri. Does anyone know any of the Assistant United States Attorneys for the Western District of Missouri, or any other member of the staff, including support personnel?

4. You will now hear a list of individuals who may be called as witnesses in this case. If you know any of these individuals, please raise your hand when you hear that person's name called. [Read witness list.]

5. Did you know any other members of the panel before reporting for jury service? If so, please identify the panel member or members you know and describe the relationship. If both of you are chosen for the jury, is there anything about knowing another member of the jury panel that would make it difficult for you to make your own individual decision about the guilt or innocence of the defendants in this case?

6. In this case, the United States has charged . . . [Read summary of the case.] Has any member of the jury panel read, heard, or seen anything about these charges?

7. Have any of you ever served on a trial jury, either in state or federal court? [If there are any affirmative responses, the following questions are proposed:

(a) What kind of case?
(b) Did the jury reach a verdict?
(c) Is there anything about your prior jury service that would make you unable to be fair and impartial to both sides of this case?]

8. Have any of you ever served on a grand jury in state or federal court?

9. Do you have any family members in law enforcement? If so, what agency or department? In what capacity? Is there anything in that employment experience that would make you unable to be fair and impartial to both sides of this case?

10. Have you or any of your family members ever received any legal training or been employed in a law office? Tell me about the nature of the training or employment? Is there anything about that educational or employment experience that would make you unable to be fair and impartial to both sides of this case?

11. Have you or any of your family members ever been involved in any disputes or litigation with the United States Government, including

the Internal Revenue Service? Describe the nature of the dispute or litigation. Is there anything about that experience that would make you unable to be fair and impartial to both sides of this case?

12. Does anyone hold negative opinions about the federal government or any of its agencies such as the IRS or SEC?

13. Have you or any of your family members ever been arrested, charged, or convicted of a serious criminal offense? Tell us more. Is there anything about that experience that would make you unable to be fair and impartial to both sides of this case?

14. Have you or any of your family members ever been a victim of a crime? Please describe. Is there anything about that experience that would make you unable to be fair and impartial to both sides of this case?

15. Have you or any of your family members ever been a witness at trial? Is there anything about that experience that would make you unable to be fair and impartial to both sides of this case?

16. Have you or any of your family members ever had a bad experience in court or with lawyers?

17. The Court will instruct you as to witness's credibility. One or more law enforcement officers may testify in this case. Would any member of the jury panel give more credit to the testimony of a law enforcement officer than to any other witness? Would any member of the jury panel give less credit to the testimony of a law enforcement officer than to any other witness?

18. The members of the jury are required to render a judgment on whether the defendant is guilty or not guilty of the charges. Is there anyone who has religious or philosophical beliefs that would make it difficult to sit in judgment on the guilt or innocence of another person?

19. A juror is bound by the legal instructions the Court provides and cannot substitute his or her own notions of what he or she thinks the law is or should be. Is there anyone who could not or would not accept the duty to follow the law based on the instructions the Court gives to the jury?

20. The law does not permit jurors to be governed by sympathy, prejudice, or public opinion. The parties expect that jurors will carefully and impartially consider all the evidence in this case, follow the law as stated by the Court, and reach a just verdict regardless of the consequences. Is there anyone who could not or would not do that in this case?

Respectfully submitted,

John F. Biden
United States Attorney

By:
/s/ Daniel W. Hays
Daniel W. Hays
Assistant United States Attorney

/s/ Kathleen D. Whitworth
Kathleen D. Whitworth
Assistant United States Attorney

IN THE UNITED STATES DISTRICT COURT FOR THE WESTERN DISTRICT OF MISSOURI CENTRAL DIVISION

UNITED STATES OF AMERICA,	)	
	)	
Plaintiff,	)	
	)	
v.	)	No. 20-cr-0501-BCK
	)	
	)	
PARIS MARSHALL,	)	
	)	
Defendant.	)	

GOVERNMENT'S PROPOSED WITNESS LIST

COMES NOW the United States of America, by and through John F. Biden, United States Attorney, and Daniel W. Hays and Kathleen D. Whitworth, Assistant United States Attorneys, all for the Western District of Missouri, and files with this Honorable Court its witness list.

[List government witnesses who may be called at trial.]

Respectfully submitted,

John F. Biden
United States Attorney

By:
/s/ Daniel W. Hays
Daniel W. Hays
Assistant United States Attorney

/s/ Kathleen D. Whitworth
Kathleen D. Whitworth
Assistant United States Attorney

IN THE UNITED STATES DISTRICT COURT FOR THE WESTERN DISTRICT OF MISSOURI CENTRAL DIVISION

UNITED STATES OF AMERICA,	)	
	)	
Plaintiff,	)	
	)	
v.	)	No. 20-cr-0501-BCK
	)	
	)	
PARIS MARSHALL,	)	
	)	
Defendant.	)	

GOVERNMENT'S PROPOSED EXHIBIT LIST

COMES NOW the United States of America, by and through John F. Biden, United States Attorney, and Daniel W. Hays and Kathleen D. Whitworth, Assistant United States Attorneys, all for the Western District of Missouri, and files with this Honorable Court its exhibit list.

[List government exhibits that may be introduced at trial.]

Respectfully submitted,

John F. Biden
United States Attorney

By:
/s/ Daniel W. Hays
Daniel W. Hays
Assistant United States Attorney

/s/ Kathleen D. Whitworth
Kathleen D. Whitworth
Assistant United States Attorney

IN THE UNITED STATES DISTRICT COURT FOR THE WESTERN DISTRICT OF MISSOURI CENTRAL DIVISION

UNITED STATES OF AMERICA,	)	
	)	
Plaintiff,	)	
	)	
v.	)	No. 20-cr-0501-BCK
	)	
	)	
PARIS MARSHALL,	)	
	)	
Defendant.	)	

GOVERNMENT'S PROPOSED JURY INSTRUCTIONS

COMES NOW the United States of America, by and through John F. Biden, United States Attorney, and Daniel W. Hays and Kathleen D. Whitworth, Assistant United States Attorneys, all for the Western District of Missouri, and respectfully submits the proposed jury instructions listed below and attached hereto, for use in the trial of this matter. The United States reserves the right to supplement these proposed instructions as required to meet additional issues which may arise at trial.

Respectfully submitted,

John F. Biden
United States Attorney

By:
/s/ Daniel W. Hays
Daniel W. Hays
Assistant United States Attorney

/s/ Kathleen D. Whitworth
Kathleen D. Whitworth
Assistant United States Attorney

[Instructions similar to the ones submitted by the defense to be inserted here.]

Tab 4 Jury Selection

Ideal Jurors for Ms. Paris Marshall:

Military Background

Older

Financially Illiterate

Rural

Ideal Jurors for the U.S. Government:

College Educated

Professional

Financially Literate

Younger

Investors

Urban

Tab 5 Opening Statement

Opening Statement for Ms. Marshall:

May it please the Court. Ladies and gentlemen, I am Marion Maughmer. Along with Mr. Russell Knox, we speak for Ms. Marshall. There will be no evidence in this case that will establish Ms. Marshall intended to defraud anyone. In fact, you will soon see that she never conspired to commit fraud or securities law violations, or any of the other alleged offenses of the conspiracy. Also, the evidence will show that she never committed any of the substantive acts alleged, or aided or abetted in the commission of those crimes. In short, she believed in the American Banking Corporation and dedicated years of her life to making that corporation a success for its investors and customers. *She is a victim of fraud, not a fraudster*. She never detected anything was out of line. She is innocent of the charges.

Did fraud occur in this case? Yes. Was Ms. Marshall aware of the misdeeds of others? Absolutely not. *She is a victim of fraud, not a fraudster.*

Ms. Marshall is very different from the others being charged here. She is the only woman charged. She also is the only defendant who resides in Colorado, where she was born and raised. After graduating from Washington Park High School, she enlisted in the U.S. Air Force and served in security forces, guarding the gates of Hanscom AFB, Massachusetts, Hill AFB, Utah, and Ramstein AFB, Germany. She served a total of 15 years on active duty before separating under Honorable Conditions. Once she completed five years of reservist duty, she retired.

You will learn that Ms. Marshall met her husband, John, in Germany and that the two of them have three children, ages 7, 10, and 13. John retired from active-duty military service six years ago and now works as a nurse at Children's Hospital.

After being a stay-at-home mother for almost a decade, Ms. Marshall was recruited to work at American Banking Corp. by her best friend, Susie Johnson. There, Ms. Marshall worked diligently in the accounting department, kept meticulous records, and responded to email correspondence when investors had questions.

We anticipate the government will produce over a thousand exhibits during this six-week trial. There will not be one document pointing to any culpability of Ms. Marshall. In fact, you will see that these documents will exonerate Ms. Marshall. Let's look at this timeline of Ms. Marshall's employment with American Banking. [Discuss.]

Remember, the Government has the burden of proving guilt beyond a reasonable doubt, which is a very high standard. Hold the government to that high burden. Please keep an open mind until all the evidence has been presented and go back into that deliberation room to discuss with your fellow jurors.

Ms. Marshall is counting on you to evaluate the evidence fairly. We believe you will clearly see by the end of this trial that *she is a victim of fraud, not a fraudster*. We believe you will find her Not Guilty of participating in the charged conspiracy and Not Guilty of the remaining fraud charges.

Thank you.

Tab 6 Government's Case

[Insert witness notes and cross examination material here.]

Tab 7 Motion for Judgment of Acquittal at Close of Government's Case

IN THE UNITED STATES DISTRICT COURT FOR THE WESTERN DISTRICT OF MISSOURI CENTRAL DIVISION

UNITED STATES OF AMERICA,	)	
	)	
Plaintiff,	)	
	)	
v.	)	No. 20-cr-0501-BCK
	)	
	)	
PARIS MARSHALL,	)	
	)	
Defendant.	)	

MS. MARSHALL'S MOTION FOR JUDGMENT OF ACQUITTAL AT THE CLOSE OF GOVERNMENT'S CASE

COMES NOW Ms. Paris Marshall, by and through her attorneys, hereby moves that this Honorable Court, pursuant to Federal Rule of Criminal Procedure 29(a), to enter judgment of acquittal on behalf of Ms. Marshall. After the government closes its evidence, the Court on Ms. Marshall's motion must enter a judgment of acquittal of any offense for which the evidence is insufficient to sustain a conviction. Ms. Marshall states the prosecution has failed to introduce sufficient evidence to prove that Ms. Marshall is guilty beyond a reasonable doubt of any of the counts charged in the indictment. Based on the reasons set forth in this Motion and the Memorandum of Support attached hereto, it is requested that the Court enter judgment of acquittal on behalf of Ms. Marshall as to Counts 1, 2, 9, 10, 11, 12, 13, and 14.

Dated: November 16, 2022 Respectfully Submitted,

JOHNSON, SMITH & SHOOK L.L.P.

By /s/ Russell K. Knox
Russell K. Knox #567892

Marion J. Maughmer #456214
10000 Highland Street
Jefferson City, Missouri 65101
Phone: (573) 980-0000

ATTORNEYS FOR MS. MARSHALL

[Insert MEMORANDUM OF SUPPORT here.]

Tab 8 Marshall's Case

[Insert direct examination questions for witnesses here.]

Tab 9 Motion for Judgment of Acquittal at Close of All Evidence

IN THE UNITED STATES DISTRICT COURT FOR THE WESTERN DISTRICT OF MISSOURI CENTRAL DIVISION

UNITED STATES OF AMERICA,	)	
	)	
Plaintiff,	)	
	)	
v.	)	No. 20-cr-0501-BCK
	)	
	)	
PARIS MARSHALL,	)	
	)	
Defendant.	)	

MS. MARSHALL'S MOTION FOR JUDGMENT OF ACQUITTAL AT THE CLOSE OF ALL THE EVIDENCE

COMES NOW Ms. Paris Marshall, by and through her attorneys, hereby moves that this Honorable Court, pursuant to Federal Rule of Criminal Procedure 29(a), to enter judgment of acquittal on behalf of Ms. Marshall. After the government close of all the evidence, the Court on Ms. Marshall's motion must enter a judgment of acquittal of any offense for which the evidence is insufficient to sustain a conviction. Ms. Marshall states the prosecution has failed to introduce sufficient evidence to prove that Ms. Marshall is guilty beyond a reasonable doubt of any of the counts charged in the indictment. Based on the reasons set forth in this Motion and the Memorandum of Support attached hereto, it is requested that the Court enter judgment of acquittal on behalf of Ms. Marshall as to Counts 1, 2, 9, 10, 11, 12, 13, and 14.

Dated: November 16, 2022

Respectfully Submitted,
JOHNSON, SMITH & SHOOK L.L.P.

By /s/ Russell K. Knox
Russell K. Knox #567892
Marion J. Maughmer #456214

10000 Highland Street
Jefferson City, Missouri 65101
Phone: (573) 980-0000

ATTORNEYS FOR MS. MARSHALL

[Insert MEMORANDUM OF SUPPORT here.]

Tab 10 Jury Instruction Conference

[Insert final jury instructions here and notes regarding the jury instruction conference.]

Tab 11 Closing Argument

Closing Argument for Ms. Marshall:

We told you at the outset of trial that fraud was committed. You have sat through days of testimony and mountains of documents detailing that fraud. Our best estimate is that $20 million of fraud was perpetrated.

We told you at the outset that there were victims of this fraud. You now have heard from dozens who lost their life savings to American Banking Corp. fraud. They lost tuition dollars and can no longer send their kid to school. They lost their retirement savings and can no longer retire. Victims.

We also told you at the outset that Ms. Marshall is one of those victims, not a fraudster. Now that you have heard and seen all the evidence, Ms. Marshall hopes that you will determine that she is innocent of these charges and just another one of the American Banking victims, not a fraudster.

How do we know she was a victim? Let's start with the witnesses. Not one witness has walked into this courtroom to say they were defrauded by Ms. Marshall. Yes, many of them received email correspondence or letters from Ms. Marshall, but none could testify to whether she was in some kind of conspiracy to hurt others financially.

Let's look at the documents. Think about it. Ms. Marshall created most of these documents, keeping meticulous records. Does a fraudster keep a paper trail? Of course not. Fraudsters like to meet in person in an open field where no one can hear the fraudulent plan being hatched. Fraudsters like to burn or destroy records, not archive them. Ms. Marshall so believed in American Banking and its leaders that she kept detailed records so no one would lose track of their growing investments in the dream called American Banking Corp.

Ladies and gentlemen, Ms. Marshall is clearly a victim, not a fraudster. All of these corporate documents, letters, and emails have been admitted into evidence. When you get back to the jury deliberation room, you can request each and every document. Please do so. Please pour through these records. You will not find one email sent by Ms. Marshall intimating or expressly stating that the corporation is a fraud. There will be no email traffic of Ms. Marshall joking with others about cheating anyone or getting over. There is no documentation that Ms. Marshall was trying to get rich at the expense of others. The email traffic documents that she thought all investigators were getting richer together. She believed. She was deceived. She got hurt too. She is a victim. She is not a fraudster.

Let's look at the timeline I showed you in the opening. [Discuss.]

Let's now look at the jury instructions. I will place my set on the ELMO. Let me highlight the ones important to Ms. Marshall. [Discuss.]

Now being displayed is the verdict form. Here's how Ms. Marshall wants you to fill out. [Check Not Guilty in each blank with an ink pen while displaying on ELMO.]

You have been so patient with us lawyers during these last several weeks. We thank you for your attention to all the witnesses and the admitted documents and photographs. We know it has been a long journey.

We ask that you not tire. Your most important task is ahead. We need you to go back into that jury deliberation room and fight for Ms. Marshall. We need you to dig deep and do the right thing. Mistakes were made, victims were hurt, some got rich. But Ms. Marshall is so different from the real leaders of the criminal enterprise we now call American Banking.

She is a victim, not a fraudster.

Thank you for your time.

Index